STANDARD LEGAL FORMS AND AGREEMENTS FOR SMALL BUSINESS

Do it yourself — Save time and money

Edited by
Stephen L.P. Sanderson, LL.B. (Hons.), LL.M.

Self-Counsel Press Inc.
a subsidiary of
International Self-Counsel Press Ltd.
Canada U.S.A.
(Printed in Canada)

Printed in Canada

First edition: April, 1990
Reprinted: April, 1991; October, 1993

Cataloging in Publication Data
Standard legal forms and agreements for small business

    (Self-counsel legal series)
    ISBN 0-88908-925-6

1. Business - Forms.   2. Small business - Forms.   3. Contracts.
I. Sanderson, Stephen L.P.   II. Series.
    HF5371.S722 1990 651'.29 C90-091047-X

Cover props courtesy of Willson/Williams & Mackie Ltd.

Self-Counsel Press Inc.
a subsidiary of
International Self-Counsel Press Ltd.

1481 Charlotte Road
North Vancouver, British Columbia
V7J 1H1

1704 N. State Street
Bellingham, Washington
98225

CONTENTS

INTRODUCTION

This book is a manual of standard business and legal forms designed to save you time and money drawing up letters and documents in your business and personal affairs.

Most of the forms and their accompanying notes were drafted by practising professionals and are based on common law principles applicable throughout most of North America.

Please note: The purpose of this compilation is to provide a ready source of written forms for use in standard, unambiguous situations. Laws vary from jurisdiction to jurisdiction and specific situations may involve disputed crucial facts or special legal considerations.

An attorney should be consulted for legal advice in any case of doubt as to proper use of a form in a specific situation. It is your responsibility to determine whether you need legal advice in connection with the use of a form but, even when you decide to seek legal advice, the form will provide a time-saving basis for the consultation.

a. HOW TO USE THIS BOOK

The forms in this book are grouped by subject and numbered within each chapter. You can easily find the form you want by referring to the Table of Contents at the front of the book.

Guidelines on the purpose and use of the forms are given at the beginning of each chapter. Further instructions are printed on the forms themselves where needed. Some forms, such as the various letter setups (chapter 1) and the Employment Warning Notice (chapter 4), are shown as samples. You will want to type your own

forms using the information in the samples, but adapting them for your specific needs. Other forms, such as the Agreement of Purchase and Sale (chapter 2) and other standard contracts, can be photocopied or quickprinted and then filled in. There are many forms that you will want multiple copies of, and some that you may only use once.

b. NOTES ON FORMALITIES

1. Seals

Many of the forms are drafted to be given or executed "under seal." To "seal" a document, the common practice today is to place a small red sticker or wafer next to the signature of the people executing it. This is a holdover from the days when wax impressions were used to record a person's personal seal of promise. Red wafers, or seals, are available in most stationery stores. If you do not have a ready supply of little red seals, just have the person signing draw a little circle around the little "s" at the end of the signature line for the desired effect.

2. Corporate signatures

The normal contracts/covenants have been mainly drafted in contemplation of execution by individuals. If something has to be executed by or on behalf of a corporation, use the formal corporate signature setup in Form 103.

It is possible to bind a corporation on the individual signature of someone authorized to sign on behalf of the corporation, but it should be clearly stated that the individual is signing on behalf of the corporation and not in his or her own personal capacity.

Using the formal corporate setup makes this abundantly clear. Actually affixing the corporate seal to the signature line is desirable but not absolutely necessary.

c. WHEN YOU NEED OTHER FORMS

General office forms can be found in the Self-Counsel book, *Ready-to-use Business Forms*, which contains forms pertaining to general office procedures, personnel, sales, purchasing, accounting, and graphics. The forms are intended to be photocopied on your own letterhead and filled in.

Self-Counsel Press also publishes a variety of other forms, with accompanying instructional books, that you may find useful. A complete list and order form can be found at the back of this book.

1
DOCUMENT SETUPS

Form 100. Full block letter style

This sample illustrates the full block style of letter setup.

Form 101. Semi-block letter style

This sample illustrates the semi-block style of letter setup.

Form 102. Memorandum setup

This sample illustrates a setup for internal office memoranda.

Form 103. Formal corporate signature setup

This sample illustrates how to set up a formal corporate signature line on a contract. No independent witness is required for a corporate seal signature because the seal is the corporation's signature and the witness is the officer signing the impression of the seal. The "c/s" refers to and reminds you to impress the corporate seal of the company.

January 1, 199-

Any Company Ltd.
12 Any Street
Anytown, Anystate
12345

Attention: John H. Doe, President

Dear Sir:

Re Full Block Letter Style

Further to your query, we use what is commonly known as a "full block" style of letter setup for use with a printed letterhead.

As this letter demonstrates, each part of the letter begins flush with the left-hand margin.

The choice of letter set up may be affected by the physical limitations of your printed letterhead. However, other things being equal, the "full block" style of letter setup is the easiest to type.

In closing, please note that this letter is composed in the first person plural ("we") as though it comes from our business rather than from any particular individual. This means that the signature line should reflect the business as well.

Very truly yours,

Acme Letter-Writing Inc.

by:

R.J. Roe, Customer Relations

copy to Customer Records
RR/ss

FORM 100

Acme Letter-Writing Inc.
1 Any Road
Anycity, Anystate
12345

January 1, 199-

Jane L. Doe
12 Home Street
Anytown, Anystate
45678

Dear Ms. Doe:

Re Semi-Block Letter Style

Further to your query, I use what is commonly known as a "semi-block" style of letter setup.

As you can see from this letter, the inside address and opening salutation begin flush with the left-hand margin.

However, the date and any return address (where you are not using a printed letterhead) are typed in the upper right-hand corner. Also, the first line of each paragraph is indented and the complimentary closing and any underlined subject line between the opening salutation and the first paragraph are usually centered.

I use the "semi-block" style of letter setup because it most closely resembles the way I was taught to write a letter by hand.

In closing, please note that I have composed this letter in the first person singular ("I") as though it comes specifically from me rather than from my business. This means that the signature should emphasize me as well.

Very truly yours,

Richard J. Roe

RJR/ss

FORM 101

MEMORANDUM

To:

From:

Date:

Subject:

FORM 102

FORMAL CORPORATE SIGNATURE

_____
(full corporate name)

by:_____c/s
(signer's name, office)

for example:

ACME LETTER WRITING INC.

by:_____c/s
Richard J. Roe, President

FORM 103

2
NEW BUSINESSES

Form 200. Proposal to buy a business

You may want to find out whether the owner of a business is prepared to sell it in principle before going to the time and trouble of making a formal, potentially legally binding, offer. Use this form to sound out a proposal to purchase a business. Fill in the forms with the pertinent information.

Form 201. Agreement of purchase and sale of business assets (with full warranties)

Use this form, with proper legal and accounting advice, to make a formal offer for the purchase and sale of the assets of a business. Note that the allocation of the total purchase price between the specific assets may have significant tax consequences for both parties. Note also the wide warranty protection in the agreement, which is to the advantage of the purchaser.

In section 1.02, list exclusions (e.g., cash on hand or on deposit, accounts receivable, book and other debts due or accruing due).

In section 6.01, fill in vendor or purchaser as agreed between parties.

Form 202. Agreement of purchase and sale of business assets (with limited warranties)

Use this form, with proper legal and accounting advice, to prepare a formal agreement of purchase and sale of business assets with limited warranty protection for the benefit of the purchaser. Note that the allocation of the total purchase price between the specific assets may have significant tax consequences for both parties.

Note also the limitations of warranties as to quality and fitness for purpose and the non-survival of all warranties, which is to the advantage of the vendor.

In section 1.02, list exclusions (e.g., cash on hand or on deposit, accounts receivable, book and other debts due or accruing due).

In section 6.01, fill in vendor or purchaser as agreed between parties.

Form 203. Agreement of purchase and sale of shares

There are two ways to buy a business owned by a corporation: by buying the assets of the business and by buying the corporation itself. The disadvantages of buying the corporation is that you are acquiring a package of assets and liabilities. You can ask for warranties from the vendor about liabilities, but the simple fact of the matter is that it is impossible to independently check out all the potential liabilities. On the other hand, the purchase of a corporation may have certain income tax advantages. Use this form, with proper accounting and legal advice, to prepare a simple agreement for the purchase and sale of the shares of a corporation.

Form 204. Partnership agreement

Use this form, with proper legal advice, to prepare a simple partnership agreement between two or more partners. It is important to realize that partnership, like marriage, should not be entered into lightly. Partners have wide apparent authority to personally bind the other partners. Note, however, that a partnership agreement only governs the relationship between the partners, and limitations on a partner's actual authority will probably not affect dealings with third parties who have no knowledge of the terms of the partnership agreement. Nonetheless, there is great value in spelling out the relationship between the partners.

Form 205. Joint venture agreement

Use this form, with proper legal advice, to prepare a formal joint venture agreement between two or more partners. Note that a joint venture is, in law, a partnership for a particular venture.

(See guidelines for Form 204.)

Form 206. Partnership agreement checklist

Use the checklist on this form to map out a proposed partnership agreement.

Form 207. Distribution agreement

Use this form with proper legal advice, to draft a distribution agreement for the supply and re-sale of specific products.

Note that the form is set up for corporate signatures (with a personal guarantee provision for the individual behind the distributor corporation) but you can set it up for an individual distributor signature and delete the references to guarantee.

Form 208. Commission sales agreement

Use this form, with proper legal advice, to draft a commission sales agreement where an agent agrees to sell specific products on behalf of a principal for a commission.

Form 209. Business plan checklist

Prior to seeking any major financing for a business, it is a good idea to prepare a business plan. It should set out in detail what the business is about and how the principals expect to accomplish their short- and long-term goals. It often becomes part of the financing contract. Use this form to ensure that your business plan is complete. For more information on business plans, see *Preparing a Successful Business Plan*, another title in the Self-Counsel Series.

PROPOSAL TO BUY A BUSINESS

January 1, 199-
Any Company Ltd.
12 Any Street
Anytown, Anystate
12345

Attention: John Doe

Dear Mr. Doe

Re Purchase of _____
_____*(name of business)*

We are interested in negotiating an agreement for the purchase and sale as a going concern of all the business assets, including furniture, fixtures, and equipment, stock in trade, parts and supplies, leasehold interest, and goodwill, owned by you in connection with the

_____
_____*(type of business)*
business carried on as_____
_____*(name of business)*
at _____
_____*(address)*

Subject to formal contract, we are prepared to pay $_____ for the business on the following terms:

If you are interested in selling at this price on these terms, please let us know and we will make you a formal offer to purchase.

Very truly yours,

_____
_____*(signature)*

FORM 200

8

AGREEMENT OF PURCHASE AND SALE OF BUSINESS ASSETS
(WITH FULL WARRANTIES)

This agreement of purchase and sale is made in two original copies between

(1)_____
(the "Vendor")

and

(2) _____
(the "Purchaser")

SUBJECT MATTER

1.01 The Purchaser agrees to buy and the Vendor agrees to sell to the Purchaser as a going concern all the undertaking and assets owned by the Vendor in connection with the

_____
(type of business)

business carried on as_____
(name of business)

at _____
(address)

(the "business") including, without limiting the generality of the foregoing:

a) the furniture, fixtures, and equipment more particularly described in Schedule A (the "equipment");

b) all saleable stock in trade (the "stock in trade");

c) all useable parts and supplies (the "parts and supplies");

d) all leasehold interest in the lease held by the Vendor from (name of landlord) (the "lease");

e) the goodwill of the business together with the exclusive right to the Purchaser to represent itself as carrying on business in succession to the Vendor and to use the business style of the business and variations in the business to be carried on by the Purchaser (the "goodwill").

1.02 The following assets are expressly excluded from the purchase and sale:

FORM 201

9

PURCHASE PRICE

2.01 The purchase price payable for the undertaking and assets agreed to be bought and sold is the total of the amounts computed and allocated as follows:

a) for the equipment - $_____;

b) for the stock in trade, its direct cost to the Vendor;

c) for the parts and supplies, their direct cost to the Vendor;

d) for the goodwill - $_____;

e) for all other assets agreed to be bought and sold - $1.

2.02 The purchase price for the stock in trade shall be established by an inventory taken and valued after close of business on the day before the day of closing. The Vendor shall produce evidence satisfactory to the Purchaser of the direct cost to the Vendor of items included in stock in trade. The Purchaser may exclude from the purchase and sale any items which the Purchaser reasonably considers unsaleable by reason of defect in quality or in respect of which the Purchaser is not reasonably satisfied as to proof of direct cost.

2.03 The purchase price for the parts and supplies shall be established by an inventory taken and valued after close of business on the day before the day of closing. The Vendor shall produce evidence satisfactory to the Purchaser of the direct cost to the Vendor of items included in the parts and supplies. The Purchaser may exclude from the purchase and sale any items which the Purchaser reasonably considers unuseable or in respect of which the Purchaser is not reasonably satisfied as to proof of direct cost.

TERMS OF PAYMENT

3.01 The Vendor acknowledges receiving a check for $_____from the Purchaser on execution of this agreement to be held as a deposit by the Vendor on account of the purchase price of the undertaking and assets agreed to be bought and sold and as security for the Purchaser's due performance of this agreement.

3.02 The balance of the purchase price for the undertaking and assets agreed to be bought and sold shall be paid, subject to adjustments, by certified check on closing.

3.03 The balance of the purchase price due on closing shall be specially adjusted for all prepaid and assumed operating expenses of the business including but not limited to rent and utilities.

CONDITIONS, REPRESENTATIONS, AND WARRANTIES

4.01 In addition to anything else in this agreement, the following are conditions of completing this agreement in favor of the Purchaser:

a) that the Purchaser obtain financing on terms satisfactory to it to complete the purchase;

b) that the carrying on of the business at its present location is not prohibited by land use restrictions;

c) that the lessor of the lease consents to its assignment to the Purchaser;

FORM 201

d) that the Purchaser obtain all the permits and licenses required for it to carry on the business;

e) that the Vendor supply or deliver on closing all of the closing documents.

4.02 The following representations and warranties are made and given by the Vendor to the Purchaser and expressly survive the closing of this agreement. The representations are true as of the date of this agreement and will be true as of the date of closing when they shall continue as warranties according to their terms. At the option of the Purchaser, the representations and warranties may be treated as conditions of the closing of this agreement in favor of the Purchaser. However, the closing of this agreement shall not operate as a waiver or otherwise result in a merger to deprive the Purchaser of the right to sue the Vendor for breach of warranty in respect of any matter warranted, whether or not ascertained by the Purchaser prior to closing:

a) the Vendor owns and has the right to sell the items listed in Schedule A;

b) the assets agreed to be bought and sold are sold free and clear of all liens, encumbrances, and charges;

c) the equipment is in good operating condition;

d) the undertaking and assets agreed to be bought and sold will not be adversely affected in any material respect in any way, whether by the Vendor or by any other person or cause whatsoever, up to closing and the Vendor will carry on business as usual until closing and not do anything before or after closing to prejudice the goodwill;

e) the financial statements for the business produced by the Vendor and appended as Schedule B are fair and accurate and prepared in accordance with generally accepted accounting principles;

f) the lease is in good standing and the Vendor has fulfilled all of its obligations under the lease;

g) the Vendor has made full and fair disclosure in all material respects of any matter that could reasonably be expected to affect the Purchaser's decision to purchase the undertaking and assets agreed to be bought and sold on the terms set out in this agreement;

h) the Vendor will execute such assignments, consents, clearances, or assurances after closing, prepared at the Purchaser's expense, as the Purchaser considers necessary or desirable to assure the Purchaser of the proper and effective completion of this agreement.

RISK

5.01 The risk of loss or damage to the undertaking and assets agreed to be bought and sold remains with the Vendor until closing.

5.02 In the event of loss or damage to the tangible assets agreed to be bought and sold prior to closing, at the option of the Purchaser, the replacement cost of the assets lost or damaged or any of them may be deducted from the total purchase price otherwise payable by the Purchaser under this agreement and the corresponding lost or damaged assets shall be excluded from the purchase and sale.

FORM 201

SALES TAXES

6.01 The _____ shall pay any and all sales taxes payable in respect of the purchase and sale of assets pursuant to this agreement.

6.02 The Vendor shall pay all sales taxes payable or collectible in connection with carrying on the business up to closing and obtain and supply the Purchaser with satisfactory proof of payment within a reasonable time of closing.

NON-COMPETITION

7.01 The Vendor covenants with the Purchaser that, in consideration of the closing of this agreement, the Vendor will not operate a_____

(type of business)

business or in any way aid and assist any other person to operate such a business in

_____

(geographical area)

for a period of _____ from the date of closing.

BULK SALES

8.01 This agreement shall be completed and the Vendor agrees to comply with any applicable laws governing the sale in bulk of the stock in trade or of any of the other assets pursuant to this agreement.

CLOSING DOCUMENTS

9.01 The Vendor shall deliver to the Purchaser, in registrable form where applicable, the following closing documents (the "closing documents,") prepared or obtained at the Vendor's expense, on or before closing:

a) duplicate, properly executed Bills of Sale of the equipment, stock in trade, and parts and supplies together with evidence satisfactory to the Purchaser that the sale complies with any laws governing the sale in bulk of the stock in trade or of the sale of any of the other assets pursuant to this agreement;

b) all records and financial data, including but not limited to any list of customers and suppliers, relevant to the continuation of the business by the Purchaser;

c) a duly executed notice in proper form revoking any registration of the style of the business under any business name registration law;

d) an executed assignment of the lease to the Purchaser endorsed with the lessor's consent to the assignment;

e) such other assignments, consents, clearances, or assurances as the Purchaser reasonably considers necessary or desirable to assure the Purchaser of the proper and effective completion of this agreement.

FORM 201

MISCELLANEOUS

11.01 In this agreement, the singular includes the plural and the masculine includes the feminine and neuter and vice versa unless the context otherwise requires.

11.02 The capitalized headings in this agreement are only for convenience of reference and do not form part of or affect the interpretation of this agreement.

11.03 If any provision or part of any provision in this agreement is void for any reason, it shall be severed without affecting the validity of the balance of the agreement.

11.04 Time is of the essence of this agreement.

11.05 There are no representations, warranties, conditions, terms, or collateral contracts affecting the transaction contemplated in this agreement except as set out in this agreement.

11.06 This agreement binds and benefits the parties and their respective heirs, executors, administrators, personal representatives, successors, and assigns.

11.07 This agreement is governed by the laws of the State of _____ .

ACCEPTANCE

12.01 This agreement executed on behalf of the Purchaser constitutes an offer to purchase which can only be accepted by the Vendor by return of at least one originally accepted copy of agreement to the Purchaser on or before _____ , failing which, the offer becomes null and void. If this offer becomes null and void or is validly revoked before acceptance or this agreement is not completed by the Purchaser for any valid reason, any deposit tendered with it on behalf of the Purchaser shall be returned without penalty or interest.

Executed under seal on_____ .
                                  (date)

Signed, sealed, and	)	
delivered in the presence	)	
of:	)	
	)	
	)	
_____	)	_____ s
(signature of witness)	)	*(signature of purchaser)*
for the Purchaser	)	Purchaser
	)	
_____	)	_____ s
(signature of witness)	)	*(signature of vendor)*
for the Vendor	)	Vendor

FORM 201

AGREEMENT OF PURCHASE AND SALE OF BUSINESS ASSETS
(WITH LIMITED WARRANTIES)

This agreement of purchase and sale is made in two original copies between

(1)_____
                  (the "Vendor")

and

(2)_____
                  (the "Purchaser")

SUBJECT MATTER

1.01 The Purchaser agrees to buy and the Vendor agrees to sell to the Purchaser as a going concern all the undertaking and assets owned by the Vendor in connection with the

_____
                  (type of business)

business carried on as_____
                                (name of business)

at _____
                  (address)

(the "business) including, without limiting the generality of the foregoing:

    a) the furniture, fixtures, and equipment more particularly described in Schedule A (the "equipment");

    b) all saleable stock in trade (the "stock in trade");

    c) all useable parts and supplies (the "parts and supplies");

    d) all leasehold interest in the lease held by the Vendor from (name of landlord) (the "lease");

    e) the goodwill of the business together with the exclusive right to the Purchaser to represent itself as carrying on business in succession to the Vendor and to use the business style of the business and variations in the business to be carried on by the Purchaser (the "goodwill").

1.02 The following assets are expressly excluded from the purchase and sale:

FORM 202

14

PURCHASE PRICE

2.01 The purchase price payable for the undertaking and assets agreed to be bought and sold is the total of the amounts computed and allocated as follows:

a) for the equipment - $_____;

b) for the stock in trade, its direct cost to the Vendor;

c) for the parts and supplies, their direct cost to the Vendor;

d) for the goodwill - $_____;

e) for all other assets agreed to be bought and sold - $1.

2.02 The purchase price for the stock in trade shall be established by an inventory taken and valued after close of business on the day before the day of closing. The Vendor shall produce evidence satisfactory to the Purchaser of the direct cost to the Vendor of items included in stock in trade. The Purchaser may exclude from the purchase and sale any items which the Purchaser reasonably considers unsaleable by reason of defect in quality or in respect of which the Purchaser is not reasonably satisfied as to proof of direct cost.

2.03 The purchase price for the parts and supplies shall be established by an inventory taken and valued after close of business on the day before the day of closing. The Vendor shall produce evidence satisfactory to the Purchaser of the direct cost to the Vendor of items included in the parts and supplies. The Purchaser may exclude from the purchase and sale any items which the Purchaser reasonably considers unuseable or in respect of which the Purchaser is not reasonably satisfied as to proof of direct cost.

TERMS OF PAYMENT

3.01 The Vendor acknowledges receiving a check for $_____ from the Purchaser on execution of this agreement to be held as a deposit by the Vendor on account of the purchase price of the undertaking and assets agreed to be bought and sold and as security for the Purchaser's due performance of this agreement. If this agreement is not completed by the Purchaser for any valid reason, the deposit shall be returned without penalty or interest.

3.02 The balance of the purchase price paid for the undertaking and assets agreed to be bought and sold shall be paid, subject to adjustments, by certified check on closing.

3.03 The balance of the purchase price due on closing shall be specially adjusted for all prepaid and assumed operating expenses of the business including but not limited to rent and utilities.

CONDITIONS, REPRESENTATIONS, AND WARRANTIES

4.01 The following are conditions of completing this agreement in favor of the Purchaser:

a) that the Vendor owns and has the right to sell the items listed in Schedule A;

b) that the assets agreed to be bought and sold are sold free and clear of all liens, encumbrances, and charges;

c) that the carrying on of the business at its present location is not prohibited by land use restrictions;

d) that the lessor of the lease consents to its assignment to the Purchaser;

FORM 202

e) that the lease is in good standing and the Vendor has fulfilled all of its obligations under the lease;

f) that the Vendor supply or deliver on closing all of the required closing documents.

4.02 The Purchaser acknowledges that it is buying the equipment as and where is without any representations or warranties as to quality or fitness for purpose.

4.03 The Purchaser further acknowledges that any representations, warranties, and conditions made or given by the Vendor in connection with this agreement operate only as conditions of closing this agreement and do not survive the closing of this agreement.

RISK

5.01 The risk of loss or damage to the undertaking and assets agreed to be bought and sold remains with the Vendor until closing.

SALES TAX

6.01 The _____ shall pay any and all sales taxes payable in respect of the purchase and sale of assets pursuant to this agreement.

BULK SALES

7.01 This agreement shall be completed and the Vendor agrees to comply with any applicable laws governing the sale in bulk of the stock in trade or of any of the other assets pursuant to this agreement.

CLOSING DOCUMENTS

8.01 The Vendor shall deliver to the Purchaser, in registrable form where applicable, the following closing documents, prepared or obtained at the Vendor's expense, on or before closing:

a) duplicate, properly executed Bills of Sale of the equipment, stock in trade, and parts and supplies together with evidence satisfactory to the Purchaser that the sale complies with any laws governing the sale in bulk of the stock in trade or of the sale of any of the other assets pursuant to this agreement;

b) any lists of customers and suppliers relevant to the continuation of the business by the Purchaser;

c) a duly executed notice in proper form revoking any registration of the style of the business under any business name registration law;

d) an executed assignment of the lease to the Purchaser endorsed with the lessor's consent to the assignment.

FORM 202

CLOSING DATE

9.01 The purchase and sale in this agreement shall close on _____

(date)

MISCELLANEOUS

10.01 In this agreement, the singular includes the plural and the masculine includes the feminine and neuter and vice versa unless the context otherwise requires.

10.02 The capitalized headings in this agreement are only for convenience of reference and do not form part of or affect the interpretation of this agreement.

10.03 If any provision or part of any provision in this agreement is void for any reason, it shall be severed without affecting the validity of the balance of the agreement.

10.04 Time is of the essence of this agreement.

10.05 There are no representations, warranties, conditions, terms, or collateral contracts affecting the transaction contemplated in this agreement except as set out in this agreement.

10.06 This agreement binds and benefits the parties and their respective heirs, executors, administrators, personal representatives, successors, and assigns.

10.07 This agreement is governed by the laws of the State of _____ .

Executed under seal on_____.

(date)

Signed, sealed, and delivered in the presence of:	))))	
	)	
_____	)	_____s
(signature of witness)	)	*(signature of purchaser)*
for the Purchaser	)	Purchaser
	)	
_____	)	_____s
(signature of witness)	)	*(signature of vendor)*
for the Vendor	)	Vendor

FORM 202

AGREEMENT OF PURCHASE AND SALE OF SHARES

This agreement of purchase and sale is made in two original copies between

(1)_____
      (the "Vendor")

and

(2)_____
      (the "Purchaser")

Whereas the Vendor owns all of the issued shares of

_____
      (the "Corporation");

It is agreed as follows:

SUBJECT MATTER

1.01 The Purchaser agrees to buy and the Vendor agrees to sell to the Purchaser all of the shares owned by the Vendor in the Corporation (the "Shares").

PURCHASE PRICE

2.01 The purchase price payable for the Shares is the total of the amounts allocated among the Shares as follows:

    a) for all the _____shares - $ _____
      (class)

    b) for all the _____ shares - $_____ etc.
      (class)

TERMS OF PAYMENT

3.01 The Vendor acknowledges receiving a check for $_____from the Purchaser on execution of this agreement to be held by the Vendor as a deposit on account of the purchase price of the Shares and as security for the Purchaser's due performance of this agreement.

3.02 The Purchaser shall pay the balance of the purchase price of the Shares by certified check on closing.

3.03 It is understood and agreed that the purchase price of the Shares is based on the financial position of the Corporation shown in the balance sheet produced by the Vendor for the Corporation and appended as Schedule A. If the net book value of the Corporation as of the date of closing is less than_____% of the net book value of the Corporation shown in Schedule A, the Vendor shall refund the Purchaser the dollar value difference within a reasonable time of receipt of written notice of the difference. For the purposes of this paragraph, the net book value of the Corporation means the dollar book value of the assets of the Corporation minus the dollar book value of the liabilities, other than for shareholder equity, of the Corporation determined in accordance with generally accepted accounting principles.

FORM 203

CONDITIONS, REPRESENTATIONS, AND WARRANTIES

4.01 In addition to anything else in this agreement, the following are conditions of completing this agreement in favor of the Purchaser:

a) that the Vendor owns all the issued shares of the Corporation;

b) that the Shares are fully paid up and non-assessable;

c) that no agreement or option exists pursuant to which the Corporation is or may be obliged to issue further shares of its authorized capital;

d) that the Shares are sold free and clear of all liens, encumbrances, and charges;

e) that any consent required for the transfer of the Shares in accordance with the Purchaser's direction is given;

f) that the Corporation is duly incorporated, validly subsisting, and in good standing under the laws of its jurisdiction of incorporation;

g) that the Corporation is not party to any collective agreement with a labor union;

h) that the Vendor give the Purchaser and all duly authorized representatives of the Purchaser full and complete access during normal business hours to the business premises and corporate, business, accounting, tax, and employment records of the Corporation for the purpose of investigating the business and affairs of the Corporation;

i) that the Purchaser obtain financing on terms satisfactory to the Purchaser to complete the purchase;

j) that the Vendor supply or deliver on closing all of the closing documents.

4.02 The Purchaser agrees that, unless and until the purchase of the Shares contemplated in this agreement is completed, the Purchaser shall keep confidential all information obtained by the Purchaser from the Vendor or the Corporation about the Vendor and the business and affairs of the Corporation.

4.03 The following representations and warranties are made and given by the Vendor to the Purchaser and expressly survive the closing of this agreement. The representations are true as of the date of this agreement and will be true as of the date of closing when they shall continue as warranties according to their terms. At the option of the Purchaser, the representations and warranties may be treated as conditions of the closing of this agreement in favor of the Purchaser. However, the closing of this agreement shall not operate as a waiver or otherwise result in a merger to deprive the Purchaser of the right to sue the Vendor for breach of warranty in respect of any matter warranted, whether or not ascertained by the Purchaser prior to closing:

a) the Articles of Incorporation and all amendments to the Articles of Incorporation of the Corporation are as stated in Schedule B;

b) the issued share capital of the Corporation is as stated in Schedule C;

FORM 203

19

c) the balance sheet appended in Schedule A and the financial statements for the last _____ complete fiscal years of the Corporation produced by the Vendor

   (number)

   appended in Schedule D have been prepared in accordance with generally accepted accounting principles applied on a consistent basis and are fair and accurate;

d) the Corporation owns the assets recorded in the balance sheet appended in Schedule A free and clear of liens, charges, and encumbrances except as noted in Schedule E;

e) the Corporation has properly reported and is not in arrears of payment of any direct or indirect taxes or of any employee-related statutory deductions or remittances;

f) the corporate, business, accounting, tax, and employment records of the Corporation are complete in all material respects;

g) the business of the Corporation will not be adversely affected in any material respect in any way, whether by the Vendor or by any other person or cause whatsoever, up to closing and the Vendor will not do anything before or after closing to prejudice the goodwill of the Corporation;

h) the Corporation will carry on business as usual until closing except that it will not declare any dividends or make any other distributions of capital or retained earnings or undertake or compromise any major contractual liabilities without the express written consent of the Purchaser;

i) there are no outstanding legal actions or judgments against the Corporation and the Corporation is not in default of any agreement to which the Corporation is a party and that all such agreements are in good standing and the Corporation is entitled to all stated benefits in such agreements;

j) the Vendor has made full and fair disclosure in all material respects of any matter that could reasonably be expected to affect the Purchaser's decision to purchase the Shares on the terms set out in this agreement;

k) the Vendor will execute such assignments, consents, clearances, or assurances after closing, prepared at the Purchaser's expense, as the Purchaser considers necessary or desirable to assure the Purchaser of the proper and effective completion of this agreement.

4.04 The following warranty is made and given by the Purchaser to the Vendor in consideration of the closing of this agreement; the Purchaser will personally indemnify and save the Vendor harmless from claims on any outstanding personal guarantees given by the Vendor for the contractual obligations of the Corporation.

FORM 203

NON-COMPETITION

5.01 The Vendor covenants with the Purchaser that, in consideration of the closing of this agreement, the Vendor will not operate a_____

(type of business)

business or in any way aid and assist any other person to operate such a business in

_____

(geographical area)

for a period of _____ from the date of closing.

CLOSING DOCUMENTS

6.01 The Vendor shall deliver to the Purchaser, in registrable form where applicable, the following closing documents (the "closing documents"), prepared or obtained at the Vendor's expense on or before closing;

a) certificates of the Shares duly assigned in accordance with the direction of the Purchaser together with satisfactory proof of the giving of any consent required for the assignment;

b) all the corporate, business, accounting, tax, and employment records of the Corporation;

c) the written registration of each director and officer of the Corporation effective as of the date of closing together with each director's and officer's personal release of all contracts with and claims against the Corporation;

d) a duly certified record of a resolution passed by the shareholders of the Corporation electing_____

(name(s))

_____

to the Board of Directors of the Corporation effective as of the date of closing;

e) such other assignments, consents, clearances, or assurances as the Purchaser reasonably considers necessary or desirable to assure the Purchaser of the proper and effective completion of this agreement.

CLOSING DATE

7.01 The purchase and sale in this agreement shall close on_____.

(date)

MISCELLANEOUS

8.01 In this agreement, the singular includes the plural and the masculine includes the feminine and neuter and vice versa unless the context otherwise requires.

8.02 The capitalized headings in this agreement are only for convenience of reference and do not form part of or affect the interpretation of this agreement.

8.03 If any provision or part of any provision in this agreement is void for any reason, it shall be severed without affecting the validity of the balance of the agreement.

FORM 203

21

8.04 Time is of the essence of this agreement.

8.05 There are no representations, warranties, conditions, terms, or collateral contracts affecting the transaction contemplated in this agreement except as set out in this agreement.

8.06 This agreement binds and benefits the parties and their respective heirs, executors, administrators, personal representatives, successors, and assigns.

8.07 This agreement is governed by the laws of the State of _____.

ACCEPTANCE

9.01 This agreement executed on behalf of the Purchaser constitutes an offer to purchase which can only be accepted by the Vendor by return of at least one originally accepted copy of agreement to the Purchaser on or before _____,

(date)

failing which, the offer becomes null and void. If this offer becomes null and void or is validly revoked before acceptance or this agreement is not completed by the Purchaser for any valid reason, any deposit tendered with it on behalf of the Purchaser shall be returned without penalty or interest.

Executed under seal on _____.

(date)

Signed, sealed, and	)	
delivered in the presence	)	
of:	)	
	)	
	)	
_____	)	_____ s
(signature of witness)	)	*(signature of purchaser)*
for the Purchaser	)	Purchaser
	)	
_____	)	_____ s
(signature of witness)	)	*(signature of vendor)*
for the Vendor	)	Vendor

FORM 203

PARTNERSHIP AGREEMENT

This partnership agreement is made in_____original copies between
(number)

(1)_____
      (partner name)

(2)_____
      (partner name)

and

(3)_____
      (partner name)

(the "Partners").

PARTNERSHIP NAME AND BUSINESS

1.01 The Partners agree to carry on a business of_____
                                                          (type of business)

as partners under the name_____.
                                                 (the "Partnership")

No person may be introduced as a Partner and no other business may be carried on by the Partnership without the consent in writing of all the Partners.

1.02 The principal place of business of the Partnership for the time being is

_____.
      (address)

TERM

2.01 The Partnership begins on_____
                                            (date)

and continues until terminated in accordance with this agreement.

PARTNERSHIP SHARES AND CAPITAL

3.01 The Partners shall participate in the assets, liabilities, profits, and losses of the Partnership in the percentages beside their respective names (their "Partnership Shares"):

_____	-	_____ %
_____	-	_____ %
_____	-	_____ %
		100%

FORM 204

3.02 The Partners shall contribute a total of $_____in cash, in proportion to their respective Partnership Shares, to the start-up capital of the Partnership by no later than_____ .
(date)

3.03 If further capital is required to carry on the Partnership business, the Partners shall contribute it as required in proportion to their respective Partnership Shares.

3.04 No interest accrues on a Partner's capital contributions to the Partnership in proportion to his Partnership Share. However, if a Partner makes an actual payment or advance for the purpose of the Partnership beyond his Partnership Share (an "Additional Advance"), he is entitled to _____% per annum interest from the Partnership on the Additional Advance until refunded by the Partnership.

BANKING ARRANGEMENTS AND FINANCIAL RECORDS

4.01 The Partners shall maintain a bank account in the name of the Partnership business on which checks may be drawn only on the signature of at least _____
(number)

of the Partners.

4.02 The Partners shall at all times maintain full and proper accounts of the Partnership business accessible to each of the Partners at any time on reasonable notice.

PARTNERS' ACCOUNTS AND SALARIES

5.01 The financial records of the Partnership shall include separate income and capital accounts for each Partner.

5.02 No Partner may receive a salary for services rendered to the Partnership but the profit or loss of the Partnership business shall be periodically allocated among the Partners' separate income accounts and each of the Partners may, from time to time, withdraw against a credit balance in his income account.

5.03 The capital accounts of the Partners shall be maintained in proportion to their respective Partnership Shares.

5.04 No Partner shall draw down his capital account without the previous consent in writing of the other Partners. If a Partner draws down his capital account below his Partnership Share, he shall bring it up to his Partnership Share on the demand of any of the Partners.

MANAGEMENT OF PARTNERSHIP BUSINESS

6.01 Each Partner may take part in the management of the Partnership business.

6.02 Any difference arising in the ordinary course of carrying on the Partnership business shall be decided by the Partners having a majority of the Partnership Shares.

FORM 204

PARTNERS' DUTIES AND RESTRICTIONS

7.01 Each Partner shall devote substantially all of his ordinary working time to carrying on the business of the Partnership.

7.02 Each Partner shall at all times duly and punctually pay and discharge his separate debts and liabilities and shall save harmless the property of the Partnership and the other Partners from those separate debts and liabilities and, if necessary, shall promptly indemnify the other Partners for their share of any actual payment or discharge of his separate debts and liabilities by the Partnership.

7.03 No Partner shall assign or encumber his share or interest in the Partnership without the previous consent in writing of the other Partners.

7.04 No Partner shall bind the Partnership or the other Partners for anything outside the ordinary course of carrying on the Partnership business.

FISCAL YEAR END

8.01 The fiscal year end of the Partnership shall be_____

(month and day)

in each year.

TERMINATION OF PARTNERSHIP

9.01 The Partnership may be dissolved at any time during the joint lives of the Partners by a Partner giving notice in writing to the other Partners of his intention to dissolve the Partnership, in which case the Partnership is dissolved as from the date mentioned in the notice as the date of dissolution, or, if no date of dissolution is mentioned, as from the date of communication of the notice.

9.02 The Partnership is dissolved on the death or insolvency of any of the Partners or on any of the Partners becoming a mental incompetent so found by a court of law.

9.03 On dissolution of the Partnership, subject to any contrary agreement binding the former Partners and their estates and after making any necessary adjustments in accordance with generally accepted accounting principles to allow for any debit balances in the Partners' separate capital accounts, the Partnership business shall be promptly liquidated and applied in the following order:

a) to pay the debts and liabilities of the Partnership;

b) to refund any outstanding Additional Advances, together with accrued interest;

c) to distribution of the credit balances of the Partners' separate income accounts;

d) to distribution of the credit balances of the Partner's capital accounts;

e) to distribution of any residue to the Partners in proportion to their respective Partnership Shares.

FORM 204

ARBITRATION OF DISPUTES

10.01 Any dispute between the Partners arising out of or related to this agreement and any amendments to it, whether before or after dissolution of the Partnership, shall be settled by arbitration in accordance with the rules of the American Arbitration Association in force at that time and judgment on the arbitration award may be entered in any court of competent jurisdiction.

MISCELLANEOUS

11.01 In this agreement, the singular includes the plural and the masculine includes the feminine and neuter and vice versa unless the context otherwise requires.

11.02 The capitalized headings in this agreement are only for convenience of reference and do not form part of or affect the interpretation of this agreement.

11.03 If any provision or part of any provision in this agreement is void for any reason, it shall be severed without affecting the validity of the balance of the agreement.

11.04 Time is of the essence of this agreement.

11.05 The terms of this agreement may only be amended in writing dated and signed by all the Partners.

11.06 This agreement binds and benefits the Partners and their respective heirs, executors, administrators, personal representatives, successors, and assigns.

11.07 This agreement is governed by the laws of the State of _____ .

Executed under seal on_____.
                                                                                  (date)

Signed, sealed and	)	
delivered in the presence	)	
of:	)	
_____	)	_____s
(signature of witness)	)	*(signature of partner)*
	)	
_____	)	_____s
(signature of witness)	)	*(signature of partner)*
	)	
	)	_____s
_____	)	
(signature of witness)	)	*(signature of partner)*

FORM 204

JOINT VENTURE AGREEMENT

This joint venture agreement is made in _____ original copies between
(number)

(1)_____
(Joint Venture Partner name)

(2)_____
(Joint Venture Partner name)

and

(3)_____
(Joint Venture Partner name)

(the "Joint Venture Partners").

PARTNERSHIP BUSINESS

1.01 The Joint Venture Partners agree to carry on a joint venture with regard to

_____

_____

_____
(description of venture)

as partners (the "Partnership"). No person may be introduced as a Joint Venture Partner and no other business may be carried on by the Partnership without the consent in writing of all the Joint Venture Partners.

TERM

2.01 The Partnership begins on_____and continues
(date)

until terminated in accordance with this agreement.

PARTNERSHIP SHARES AND CAPITAL

3.01 The Joint Venture Partners shall participate in the assets, liabilities, profits, and losses of the Partnership in the percentages beside their respective names (their "Partnership Shares"):

_____	-	_____%
_____	-	_____%
_____	-	_____%
		100%

FORM 205

27

3.02 The Joint Venture Partners shall contribute a total of $ _____ in cash, in proportion to their respective Partnership Shares, to the start-up capital of the Partnership by no later than_____ .

(date)

3.03 No interest accrues on a Joint Venture Partner's capital contributions to the Partnership in proportion to his Partnership Share. However, if a Joint Venture Partner makes an actual payment or advance for the purpose of the Partnership beyond his Partnership Share (an "Additional Advance"), he is entitled to _____% per annum interest from the Partnership on the Additional Advance until refunded by the Partnership.

BANKING ARRANGEMENTS AND FINANCIAL RECORDS

4.01 The Partnership shall maintain a bank account on which checks may be drawn only on the signature of the Managing Joint Venture Partner (see below) or the signatures of all the Joint Venture Partners.

4.02 The Partnership shall at all times maintain full and proper accounts of the Partnership business accessible to each of the Joint Venture Partners at any time on reasonable notice.

PARTNERS' ACCOUNTS AND SALARIES

5.01 The financial records of the Partnership shall include separate income and capital accounts for each Joint Venture Partner.

5.02 No Joint Venture Partner may receive a salary for services rendered to the Partnership but the profit or loss of the Partnership business shall be periodically allocated among the Joint Venture Partners' separate income accounts and each of the Joint Venture Partners may, from time to time, withdraw against a credit balance in his income account.

5.03 The capital accounts of the Joint Venture Partners shall be maintained in proportion to their respective Partnership Shares.

5.04 No Joint Venture Partner shall draw down his capital account without the previous consent in writing of the other Joint Venture Partners. If a Joint Venture Partner draws down his capital account below his Partnership Share of all the Joint Venture Partners' capital accounts, he shall bring it up to his Partnership Share on the demand of any of the Joint Venture Partners.

MANAGEMENT OF PARTNERSHIP BUSINESS

6.01 The management of the Partnership business is vested in a Managing Joint Venture Partner elected and removable by a majority vote of the Joint Venture partners in the Partnership.

6.02 The Managing Joint Venture Partner is not liable to the Joint Venture Partners or the Partnership for any acts or failures to act in the course of managing the Partnership business committed in good faith.

FORM 205

PARTNERS' DUTIES AND RESTRICTION

7.01 Each Joint Venture Partner shall at all times duly and punctually pay and discharge his separate debts and liabilities and shall save harmless the property of the Partnership and the other Joint Venture Partners from those separate debts and liabilities and, if necessary, shall promptly indemnify the other Joint Venture Partners for their share of any actual payment or discharge of his separate debts and liabilities by the Partnership.

7.02 No Joint Venture Partner shall assign or encumber his share or interest in the Partnership without the previous consent in writing of the other Joint Venture Partners.

7.03 No Joint Venture Partner shall bind the Partnership or the other Joint Venture Partners for anything outside the ordinary course of carrying on the Partnership business.

TERMINATION OF PARTNERSHIP

8.01 The Partnership may only be voluntarily dissolved during the joint lives of the Joint Venture Partners by mutual agreement of the Joint Venture Partners.

8.02 On voluntary dissolution of the Partnership, subject to any contrary agreement binding the former Joint Venture Partners and after making any necessary adjustments in accordance with generally accepted accounting principles to allow for any debit balances in the Joint Venture Partners' separate capital accounts, the Partnership business shall be promptly liquidated and applied in the following order:

a) to pay the debts and liabilities of the Partnership;

b) to refund any outstanding Additional Advances, together with accrued interest;

c) to distribution of the credit balances of the Joint Venture Partners' separate income accounts;

d) to distribution of the credit balances of the Joint Venture partners' separate capital accounts;

e) to distribution of any residue to the Joint Venture Partners in proportion to their respective Partnership Shares.

8.03 A Joint Venture Partner involuntarily ceases to be a Joint Venture Partner on death or insolvency or becoming a mental incompetent so found by a court of law but the Partnership continues.

8.04 On a Joint Venture Partner involuntarily ceasing to be a Joint Venture Partner, subject to any contrary agreement binding the former Joint Venture Partner and the remaining Joint Venture Partners and after making any necessary adjustments in accordance with generally accepted accounting principles to allow for any debt balances in the Joint Venture Partners' separate capital accounts, the remaining Joint Venture Partners shall pay the Joint Venture Partner ceasing to be a Joint Venture Partner or his estate, as the case may be, any credit balances in his separate income and capital accounts as shown on the financial statements of the Partnership for the next month end following the date of his ceasing to be a Joint Venture Partner (the "Payment Calculation Statements") and, upon payment, the Joint Venture Partner ceasing to be a Joint Venture Partner has no further claims against the Partnership or the remaining Joint Venture Partners in respect of his interest in the Partnership. For greater certainty, the Payment Calculation Statements shall not be adjusted to show a value for goodwill or work-in-progress but shall be adjusted as though for a fiscal year end.

FORM 205

ARBITRATION OF DISPUTES

9.01 Any dispute between the Joint Venture Partners arising out of or related to this agreement and any amendments to it, whether before or after dissolution of the Partnership or a Joint Venture Partner involuntarily ceases to be a Joint Venture Partner, shall be settled by arbitration in accordance with the rules of the American Arbitration Association in force at that time and judgment on the arbitration may be entered in any court of competent jurisdiction.

MISCELLANEOUS

10.01 In this agreement, the singular includes the plural and the masculine includes the feminine and neuter and vice versa unless the context otherwise requires.

10.02 The capitalized headings in this agreement are only for convenience of reference and do not form part of or affect the interpretation of this agreement.

10.03 If any provision or part of any provision in this agreement is void for any reason, it shall be severed without affecting the validity of the balance of the agreement.

10.04 Time is of the essence of this agreement.

10.05 The terms of this agreement may only be amended in writing dated and signed by all the Joint Venture Partners.

10.06 This agreement binds and benefits the Joint Venture Partners and their respective heirs, executors, administrators, personal representatives, successors, and assigns.

10.07 This agreement is governed by the laws of the State of_____ .

Executed under seal on_____ .
(date)

Signed, sealed, and	)
delivered in the presence	)
of:	)
	)
_____	) _____s
(signature of witness)	) (signature of partner)
	)
_____	) _____s
(signature of witness)	) (signature of partner)
	)
_____	) _____s
(signature of witness)	) (signature of partner)

FORM 205

PARTNERSHIP AGREEMENT CHECKLIST

1. Name of Partnership

   _____

2. Names of Partners

   _____

   _____

   _____

   _____

   _____

   _____

3. Description of Business

   _____

   _____

   _____

   _____

4. Commencement Date

   _____

5. Term of Partnership (if any)

   _____

6. Place of Business (if any)

   _____

   _____

FORM 206

31

7.	Contributions to Capital

_____

_____

_____

_____

_____

8.	Division of Profits

_____

_____

_____

_____

9.	Fiscal Year End

_____

10.	Accounting/Valuation Principles (seek professional advice)

_____

_____

_____

_____

11.	Banking Arrangements

_____

12.	Management Duties/Decisions

_____

_____

_____

FORM 206

32

13.   Restrictions on Partners

_____

_____

_____

14.   Signing Authority

_____

_____

15.   Drawing Arrangements

_____

_____

16.   Retirement/Death Arrangements

_____

_____

17.   Non-Competition Clause?

_____

_____

18.   Admission/Expulsion of Partners

_____

_____

19.   Voluntary Dissolution of Partnership

_____

_____

20.   Dispute Arbitration Clause?

_____

_____

_____

FORM 206

DISTRIBUTION AGREEMENT

This distribution agreement is made in three original copies between

(1)_____
        (the "Supplier")

and

(2)_____
        (the "Distributor")

and is personally guaranteed by

(3)_____
        (the "Guarantor")

Whereas the Supplier wishes to market the products described in Schedule A (the "Products") through the Distributor;

It is agreed as follows:

DISTRIBUTION RIGHTS

1.01 The Supplier grants the Distributor an exclusive right to sell the Products within the territory described in Schedule B for a period of _____

commencing_____ (the "Distribution Rights").
        (date)

1.02 The Distributor shall pay the Supplier a non-refundable fee of _____ dollars ($ _____) on signing this agreement for the initial grant of the Distribution Rights.

1.03 The Distributor shall not sell or attempt to sell the Products outside of the territory described in Schedule B.

1.04 The Distributor shall use its best efforts to sell the Products for the duration of the Distribution Rights.

1.05 The Distributor may describe itself as an authorized distributor of the Products for the duration of the Distribution Rights but shall not characterize itself or enter into any transaction as an agent or in the name of the Supplier.

PRODUCT PRICES

2.01 The Supplier shall supply the Distributor with Products on the Distributor's order at the price(s), inclusive of cost of delivery to the Supplier at _____

_____
        (address)

set out in Schedule C. For greater certainty, the price(s) set out in Schedule C are quoted exclusive of any taxes and duties payable in connection with the sale which, if payable by the Supplier, may be added by the Supplier to the cost of the Products to the Distributor.

FORM 207

2.02 The Distributor shall pay the Supplier for the Products ordered from the Supplier

_____

_____

_____

_____

(terms of payment).

2.03 The Distributor may re-sell the Products at whatever price(s) the Distributor sees fit.

DEFECTIVE PRODUCTS

3.01 The Distributor may return all defective Products to the Supplier for replacement at the Supplier's expense.

3.02 The Supplier agrees to indemnify the Distributor against third-party liability incurred by selling defective Products but only to the extent that the Distributor could not have avoided or minimized the liability or damages by exercising reasonable care not to sell defective Products.

TRAINING

4.01 At the request of the Distributor, the Supplier shall train the Distributor's employees, at the Supplier's place of business and at the expense of the Distributor, in the proper use of the Products. The Supplier shall not charge the Distributor in excess of_____ _____dollars ($_____) per hour of Supplier employee time for training the Distributor's employees.

ADVERTISING AND INFORMATION MATERIALS

5.01 For the duration of the Distribution Rights, the Supplier shall furnish the Distributor, at the Supplier's cost, with reasonable quantities of advertising and user information materials to aid the Distributor in selling the Products.

PRODUCT IMAGE

6.01 Other than in the matter of pricing, the Distributor shall not do or permit anything to be done to prejudice the market image of the Products or the Supplier.

RESTRAINT OF COMPETITION

7.01 The Distributor shall not sell, or in any way assist anyone else to sell, any products that compete with the Products of the Supplier within the territory described in Schedule B for the duration of the Distribution Rights and for the calendar year immediately following termination of the Distribution Rights.

7.02 The Guarantor shall not sell, or in any way assist anyone else to sell, any products that compete with the Products of the Supplier within the territory described in Schedule B for the duration of the Distribution Rights and for the calendar year immediately following termination of the Distribution Rights.

FORM 207

SUMMARY TERMINATION OF DISTRIBUTION RIGHTS

8.01 If the Distributor breaks any term of this agreement, the Supplier may summarily terminate the Distribution Rights on notice in writing to the Distributor.

TERMINATION CONSEQUENCES

9.01 On termination of the Distribution Rights for any reason, the Distributor shall immediately cease to describe itself as an authorized distributor of the Supplier and, at the Supplier's option, the Supplier may buy back the Distributor's unsold Products or any part of them at the Distributor's cost.

ASSIGNMENT

10.01 The Distributor shall not assign the benefit of this agreement or subcontract its obligations under this agreement without the consent in writing of the Supplier, which consent may be withheld without good reason.

GUARANTEE

11.01 The Guarantor guarantees the Supplier the due performance of this agreement by the Distributor.

MISCELLANEOUS

12.01 In this agreement, the singular includes the plural and the masculine includes the feminine and neuter and vice versa unless the context otherwise requires.

12.02 The capitalized headings in this agreement are only for convenience of reference and do not form part of or affect the interpretation of this agreement.

12.03 If any provision or part of any provision in this agreement is void for any reason, it shall be severed without affecting the validity of the balance of the agreement.

12.04 Time is of the essence of this agreement.

12.05 There are no representations, warranties, conditions, terms, or collateral contracts affecting the transaction contemplated in this agreement except as set out in this agreement.

12.06 Nothing in this agreement is intended to constitute a partnership between any of the parties.

12.07 This agreement binds and benefits the parties and their respective heirs, executors, administrators, personal representatives, successors, and assigns.

FORM 207

12.08 This agreement is governed by the laws of the State of_____.

Executed under seal on_____
(date)

_____
(supplier corporate name)

by:_____c/s
(signer's name, office)

_____
(distributor corporate name)

by:_____c/s
(signer's name, office)

Signed, sealed, and   )
delivered in the presence   )
of:)
)
)
_____   ) _____s
(signature of witness)   ) *(signature of guarantor)*
for the Guarantor   )

FORM 207

COMMISSION SALES AGREEMENT

This commission sales agreement is made in two original copies between

(1)_____
　　　　　(the "Principal")

and

(2)_____
　　　　　(the "Agent")

Whereas the Principal wishes to market the product(s) described in Schedule A (the "Product(s)");

And whereas the Agent is prepared to sell the Product(s) on behalf of the Principal in return for a commission;

It is agreed as follows:

SELLING RIGHTS

1.01 The Principal grants the Agent an exclusive right to sell the Product(s) on behalf of the Principal within the territory described in Schedule B for a period of commencing_____ (the "Selling Rights").
　　　　　　　　(date)

1.02 The Agent may not sell or attempt to sell the Product(s) outside of the territory described in Schedule B.

1.03 The Agent shall use his best efforts to sell the Product(s) for the duration of the Selling Rights. At the request from time to time of the Principal, the Agent shall furnish the Principal with a reasonably detailed, written report on his efforts to sell the Product(s) in the period specified by the Principal.

1.04 The Agent shall clearly identify himself as a duly authorized sales agent of the Principal in the course of his efforts to sell the Product(s) on behalf of the Principal and may not sell the Product(s) in his own name.

PRODUCT PRICES

2.01 The Principal shall fix the selling price(s) of the Product(s) and the Agent may only sell the Product(s) at the selling price(s) fixed by the Principal.

ORDERS

3.01 The Agent shall obtain written orders for the Product(s) from buyers, signed by or on behalf of the buyers, and remit the orders to the Principal.

3.02 The Principal shall use its best efforts to fill orders duly remitted by the Agent in accordance with this agreement as expeditiously as possible.

FORM 208

COMMISSION

4.01 The Principal shall pay the Agent a commission of _____ % of the selling price, exclusive of any sales taxes, of each order or part of each order of Product(s) duly remitted by the Agent in accordance with this agreement which is paid for in full, inclusive of any sales taxes, and which is not subsequently returned for a refund.

4.02 The Principal may accept the return of Product(s) for a refund or partial refund in its sole discretion.

4.03 The Agent is not entitled to any compensation for services performed or expenses incurred in connection with this agreement other than as set out in this agreement.

TRAINING

5.01 At the request of the Agent, the Principal shall train the Agent in the proper use of the Product(s).

ADVERTISING AND INFORMATION MATERIALS

6.01 For the duration of the Selling Rights, the Principal shall furnish the Agent, at the Principal's cost, with reasonable quantities of advertising and user information materials, including demonstration Product(s), to aid the Agent in selling the Product(s).

PRODUCT IMAGE

7.01 The Agent shall not do or permit anything to be done to prejudice the market image of the Product(s) or the Principal.

RESTRAINT OF COMPETITION

8.01 The Agent shall not sell, or in any way assist anyone else to sell, any products that compete with the Product(s) of the Principal within the territory described in Schedule B for the duration of the Selling Rights and for the calendar year immediately following termination of the Selling Rights.

CONFIDENTIALITY

9.01 The Agent shall keep the Principal's business secrets, including but not limited to customer, supplier, logistical, financial, research, and development information, confidential and shall not disclose them to any third party during and after termination of the Selling Rights.

SUMMARY TERMINATION OF SELLING RIGHTS

10.01 If the Agent breaks any term of this agreement, the Principal may summarily terminate the Selling Rights on notice in writing to the Agent.

TERMINATION CONSEQUENCES

11.01 On termination of the Selling Rights for any reason, the Agent shall immediately cease to describe himself as an authorized sales agent of the Principal and cease selling the Product(s).

FORM 208

ASSIGNMENT

12.01 The Agent shall not assign the benefit of this agreement or subcontract his obligations under this agreement without the consent in writing of the Principal, which consent may be withheld without good reason.

FIDUCIARY RELATIONSHIP

13.01 The Agent accepts and acknowledges that the terms of this agreement are in addition to and do not detract from the ordinary fiduciary duties owed by the Agent to the Principal.

MISCELLANEOUS

14.01 In this agreement, the singular includes the plural and the masculine includes the feminine and neuter and vice versa unless the context otherwise requires.

14.02 The capitalized headings in this agreement are only for convenience of reference and do not form part of or affect the interpretation of this agreement.

14.03 If any provision or part of any provision in this agreement is void for any reason, it shall be severed without affecting the validity of the balance of the agreement.

14.04 Time is of the essence of this agreement.

14.05 There are no representations, warranties, conditions, terms, or collateral contracts affecting the transaction contemplated in this agreement except as set out in this agreement.

14.06 Nothing in this agreement is intended to constitute a partnership or a master and servant relationship between the parties.

14.07 This agreement binds and benefits the parties and their respective heirs, executors, administrators, personal representatives, successors and assigns.

14.08 This agreement is governed by the laws of the State of _____.

Executed under seal on_____.
(date)

Signed, sealed, and	)	
delivered in the presence	)	
of:	)	
	)	
_____	)	_____s
(signature of witness)	)	*(signature of principal)*
for the Principal	)	
	)	
	)	_____s
_____	)	
(signature of witness)	)	*(signature of commission agent)*
for the Agent	)	

FORM 208

BUSINESS PLAN CHECKLIST

A. BACKGROUND

   1. A narrative description of the development of the business or concept including the rationale for entering specific markets.

B. MANAGEMENT

   1. Resumes of the executives and senior supervisory personnel detailing:

      a)   age

      b)   academic background

      c)   shareholdings

      d)   functions

      e)   accomplishments

      f)   business references

      g)   current remuneration

   2. Availability of personnel replacements. Define to what extent the Plan is dependent on certain people.

   3. Schematic organization chart that describes the responsibilities associated with each major management position.

   4. Identify the timing and need for new management.

C. NON-MANAGEMENT WORK FORCE

   1. Identify the following:

      a)   skills required

      b)   timing of need for labor

      c)   labor availability

      d)   compensation levels

   2. Describe the fringe benefit plan and how it compares with other companies in the same geographical area and in the same industry.

   3. Current or anticipated status of union contracts, demands, and objectives with a summary of labor relations within the company. Name current and prospective unions.

   4. Availability of skilled and unskilled labor to meet company objectives.

   5. Describe labor intensity of company and labor turnover.

D. RESEARCH AND DEVELOPMENT

   1. Indicate why the product or process is unique and worthy of financial support.

FORM 209

2. Provide independent support for the product, service, or process including users reports and endorsements.

3. Comment on the state of the art domestically and internationally.

4. Comment on ability to legally protect know-how and lead time over the competition.

5. Describe anticipated research and development costs to advance prototype to production line or to improve existing production line product.

6. Describe future pressures on research and development including probable product adaptations.

E. MARKETING

1. Describe in detail the existing and proposed products or services. Submit sales literature, photographs, drawings, etc.

2. Describe the customer benefits and advantages over existing competitive products or services.

3. Define the company's marketing philosophy. Outline a detailed marketing plan which would include:

   a) analysis by product by territory
   b) optimal distribution method
   c) price structure including product line profit contribution
   d) break even analysis by product and territory
   e) market characteristics and market measurement
   f) identification of principal actual and potential customers
   g) product and package testing
   h) test marketing
   i) media selection for marketing
   j) warranty/service policy

4. Provide an analysis of competitors including an evaluation of their products, pricing, and market share.

5. Provide an estimate of market startup costs for new products.

F. MANUFACTURING

1. Provide a manufacturing plan that will identify:

   a) the need for a physical plant
   b) optimal size and layout of plant
   c) capacity of plant
   d) alternative uses
   e) burden of fixed costs and availability of a trade off of fixed costs for variable costs (i.e., sub-contracting component production)
   f) cost of the fixed assets required

FORM 209

2. The plan will provide a cost analysis that will include:

   a)   complete bill of materials costing, each naming at least two suppliers

   b)   price trends of major raw materials compared to trends in selling price of finished products

   c)   availability of all major items of raw material

3. The plan will address the following manufacturing standards:

   a)   size

   b)   weight

   c)   durability

   d)   convenience

   e)   packaging

   f)   quality

   g)   color

   h)   customer service

   i)   product standardization and compatibility

4. Comment on how plant location has been/will be determined including reference to customer proximity, supplier proximity, labor availability, transportation, etc.

5. Describe and diagram the production process.

6. Comment on production planning and scheduling procedures including an estimate of startup expenses.

7. Briefly describe existing plant and property. Comment on physical condition of plant and equipment including outstanding capital projects and probable costs of expansion.

G. LEGAL

1. Provide incorporation details:

   a)   date

   b)   jurisdiction

   c)   registered office

   d)   directors

   e)   officers

   f)   shareholders

2. Attach copies of the Incorporation Certificate.

3. Provide information on predecessor companies or partnerships including a copy of financial statements and a copy of asset and know-how transfer.

FORM 209

4. Submit a copy of:
   a)   employment contracts
   b)   pension plans including actuarial reports on extent of unfunded past service liabilities
   c)   profit sharing plans
   d)   options and warrants
   e)   patents, trademarks, industrial designs
   f)   franchise and distributorship agreements

5. Provide details on all non arm's-length relationships.

6. State whether the company's beneficial contracts are assignable. Consider licences, royalty agreements, employment contracts, leases, suppliers contracts, and collective bargaining agreements.

7. Comment on any litigation actual or contemplated as well as any changes of law that will affect the company.

8. Describe those aspects of the company's business now subject to government control and regulations.

H. FINANCIAL

1. Actual audited financial statements for the last five years if possible. Transfer to a comparative summary for ease of study.

2. Most recent interim financial statement. Ensure that all appropriate accruals are reflected in the interim.

3. Detailed cash flow and income projections should be provided for the next 36 months. All assumptions should be described. Pro-forma balance sheets should also be prepared.

4. Costs should be broken into fixed and variable components and the break-even point should be determined.

5. Whenever existing loans are outstanding identify:
   a)   lender
   b)   terms
   c)   balance
   d)   security
   e)   restrictive covenants
   f)   lending officer

FORM 209

3

SERVICES

Form 300. Engagement of services

Use this form to confirm the terms of an oral engagement of your professional or white-collar services by a client/customer. Note that the client/customer agrees to late-payment charges at the time of entering into the contract of engagement (which is required by law) and get a personal guarantee of payment for a corporate client/customer (but only where not likely to offend an established corporation).

Form 301. Engagement of another's services

Use this form to confirm the terms of an oral engagement of someone else's professional or white-collar services by your firm.

Form 302. Independent contractor agreement

Use this form, with proper legal advice, to draft a simple, blue-collar, independent contractor agreement.

Under section 1, insert general description of work.

Form 303. Authorized extras

Use this form in a blue-collar, independent contractor situation to document the authorization of extra work.

Form 304. Change work order

Use this form in a blue-collar, independent contractor situation to document agreed work changes.

ENGAGEMENT OF SERVICES

January 1, 199-

Any Company Ltd.
12 Any Street
Anytown, Anystate
12345

Dear _____

Re Terms of Engagement

This letter confirms our understanding of the terms of our engagement by _____

_____
(name of client)

    A) We will provide the following services: *(describe services)*

    B) Our charges for these services are: *(set out charges)*

    C) We will bill you: *(insert frequency or timing of billing)*

    D) Our invoices are all payable on receipt and bear interest on their unpaid amount at the rate of _____% per annum compounded annually.

    E) If the client is or becomes incorporated, the individual accepting the terms of our engagement on behalf of the client also personally guarantees payment for our services.

Please indicate your agreement to these terms by completing the acceptance on the accompanying copy of this letter and returning it to us.

Very truly yours,

_____
(signature)

The terms of engagement in this letter are accepted.

_____   ) By:_____
(date)   *(signature)*

FORM 300

ENGAGEMENT OF ANOTHER'S SERVICES

January 1, 199-

Any Company Ltd.
12 Any Street
Anytown, Anystate
12345

Dear _____

Re Terms of Engagement

This letter confirms our understanding of the terms of engagement of your services by our firm.

   A) You will provide the following services: *(describe services)*

   B) You will commence work on_____and substantially complete it by no
                                      (date)

   later than _____
                  (date)

   C) Your charges for these services will be: *(set out charges)*

If the above accords with your understanding of the terms of your engagement, please accept this letter as your authority to start work.

Any variation of the above terms, including the provision of additional services, requires our written consent.

Very truly yours,

_____
(signature)

FORM 301

INDEPENDENT CONTRACTOR AGREEMENT

This contract for services is made in two original copies between

(1)_____
                    (the "Hirer")

and

(2)_____
                    (the "Contractor")

It is agreed as follows:

1. The Contractor shall provide the Hirer with the following services as an independent contractor:

(the "Work").

2. The Contractor shall commence the Work on_____ and substantially
                                                    (date)

complete it by no later than_____ .
                              (date)

3. The total contract price (the "Contract Price") payable by the Hirer to the Contractor for doing the Work, exclusive of any Authorized Extras, is _____ dollars ($ _____).

4. Subject to any statutory holdbacks under any applicable construction or mechanics lien legislation, the Hirer shall pay the Contract Price as follows:

_____

_____

        (terms and time of payment)

5. The Contractor is only liable to perform and the Hirer is only liable to pay for extra services, in addition to the Work, that are authorized in writing setting out the price of the extra services and signed by both parties ("Authorized Extras").

6. The Contractor is entitled to interest at the rate of_____% per annum on any overdue payments for doing the Work and any Authorized Extras under this agreement.

FORM 302

7. The Contractor shall indemnify and save the Hirer harmless from any and all claims against the Hirer arising out of the performance of the Contractor's services under this agreement.

8. Time is of the essence of this agreement.

9. The terms of this agreement may only be amended in writing signed by both parties.

10. This agreement is governed by the laws of the State of_____ .

Executed under seal on_____ .
(date)

Signed, sealed, and	)	
delivered in the presence	)	
of:	)	
	)	
	)	
_____	)	_____
(signature of witness)	)	*(signature of hirer)*
for the Hirer	)	
	)	
_____	)	_____
(signature of witness)	)	*(signature of contractor)*
for the Contractor		

FORM 302

AUTHORIZED EXTRAS

Project:

Hirer:

Contractor:

Contract Date:

1. The Hirer authorizes and the Contractor agrees to do the following extra work in addition to the work set out in the above dated contract:

2. The agreed total price for the above extra work is_____dollars ($ _____).

Signed on_____
           (date)

_____   _____
(signature of hirer)   *(signature of contractor)*
the Hirer   the Contractor

FORM 303

CHANGE WORK ORDER

Project:

Hirer:

Contractor:

Contract Date:

    1. The Hirer authorizes and the Contractor agrees to make the following work changes to the above dated contract:

    2. There is no additional charge for the above changes.
OR

    2. The agreed additional charge for the above changes is _____dollars ($ _____).

Signed on_____
                         (date)

_____   _____
(signature of hirer)   *(signature of contractor)*
the Hirer   the Contractor

FORM 304

4
EMPLOYMENT

Form 400. Rejecting employment application
Use this form to deal with rejected applications for employment with your firm.

Form 401. Confirming employment terms
Use this form to document the terms of an offer of employment in secretarial or junior clerical hiring situation. Note the careful statement of annual cash salary as inclusive of statutory vacation pay and equivalent to a certain sum. When the employee is not entitled to paid vacation, this avoids any confusion as to whether weekly salary is calculated by dividing by 52 weeks or by 52 weeks less 2 weeks' vacation.

Under section b, at the end of the paragraph, list fringe benefits, or, if there are no fringe benefits, insert the following statement: "There are no fringe benefits in connection with your employment, and, in particular, there is no sick leave."

Form 402. Employment agreement
Use this form with proper legal advice to prepare a simple employment contract for more senior employees. Note the firing notice provision to limit damages for wrongful dismissal where the employee is let go or fired without good cause in law. Note also provision for a non-competition clause.

In section 2, insert list of duties in the proper space.

In section 6, list benefits at the end of the paragraph.

In section 8, if the employee is not entitled to sick leave, do not fill in the number of days and the time period; instead, insert the following statement at the end of the paragraph: "It is understood and agreed that the employee is not entitled to any paid or unpaid sick leave."

In section 10, insert type of business, geographical area, and time period in their respective places.

Form 403. Employee warning notice
Generally speaking, you cannot fire someone for incompetence without giving that person fair warning about specific problems and a reasonable opportunity to improve performance. Use this form to document the warning.

Insert description of problems requiring warning notice at the end of the first paragraph.

Insert details of requirements to improve performance at the end of the second paragraph.

Form 404. Employee dismissal letter
Firing an employee for just cause is not to be taken lightly. Use this form, with proper legal advice, to advise the employee of his or her dismissal and give reasons for it. Note that advance notice of dismissal (e.g., at the end of the week or month) or an offer of money in lieu of advance notice of dismissal may be interpreted as a waiver of your right to fire the employee for cause without notice.

Insert details of reasons for termination of employment at the end of the first paragraph.

Form 405. Employee covenants: secrecy/non-competition

Use this form, with proper legal advice, to protect your firm from employee disclosure of business secrets and departing employee competition. Restraint of competition is void as against public policy unless it is reasonable including as to length of time and geographical area of restraint. Reasonableness depends on the circumstances and customs of your industry. As a general rule, do not exceed two years for length of time (this does not mean automatically use two years) or specify a geographical area in excess of your ordinary market operations. Note that we have provided a choice of non-competition clauses, one for general competition and the other specifically for customer account competition.

Insert type of business, geographical area, and time period in their respective places in section 2.

Insert time period in proper place in section 3.

Form 406. Employee covenant: expense recovery

Use this form to obtain an enforceable employee promise to reimburse expenses disallowed as proper deductions by the tax authorities.

Form 407: Employee invention covenant

Use this form to obtain an enforceable employee acknowledgment of an employer's ownership of "employee" inventions.

January 1, 199-

Any Company Ltd.
12 Any Street
Anytown, Anystate
12345

Dear_____

Re Employment Application

Thank you for your employment application.

Unfortunately, we are unable to offer you a position with our firm at this time.

We wish you the best in your search for employment.

Very truly yours,

_____
(signature)

FORM 400

CONFIRMING EMPLOYMENT TERMS

January 1, 199-

Any Company Ltd.
12 Any Street
Anytown, Anystate
12345

Dear _____

Re Offer of Employment

This is to confirm our offer to you of a position with this firm as a _____
(position)
commencing _____ on the following terms:
(date)

   a) You will be on probation for_____weeks during which time we may terminate your employment at any time without notice or payment in lieu of notice. If your employment is continued, we may only terminate your employment without cause on two weeks' notice or payment in lieu of notice; however, we reserve the right to terminate your employment at any time without notice or payment in lieu of notice for good cause;

   b) Your gross cash salary, inclusive of any statutory vacation pay to which you may be entitled, during the probationary period of your employment is equivalent to $_____ per annum payable, subject to statutory deductions, in weekly installments not in advance; if your employment is continued, your gross cash salary, inclusive of any statutory vacation pay to which you may be entitled, will increase to the equivalent of $_____per annum also payable, subject to statutory deductions, in weekly installments not in advance; in addition, you have the following taxable fringe benefits in connection with your employment:

   OR

   There are no fringe benefits in connection with your employment and, in particular, there is no sick leave.

   c) Subject to statutory holidays, your hours of employment are _____a.m. to _____ p.m., Monday through Friday, with _____minutes off for lunch and two _____minute coffee-breaks (one to be taken in the morning and the other in the afternoon) each full working day.

FORM 401

d) You have up to_____ weeks' ordinary vacation each year; you will not receive your ordinary pay while on vacation but you will be paid any statutory vacation pay to which you are entitled; all vacation time must be reserved _____months in advance; no ordinary vacation may be taken during the first _____ months, including the probationary period, of employment.

e) You may not accumulate your time for lunches, coffee-breaks, or ordinary vacation and these must all be scheduled subject to reasonable control over timing by the firm.

f) All overtime must be expressly requested and authorized in advance by the firm; otherwise, it is worked at your own risk.

g) Your employment duties consist of:

however, this list is not to be taken as fixed or exhaustive and you will be expected to perform any reasonable employment task given by a superior.

h) You agree not to disclose any confidential information learned in the course of your employment about the business of the firm or about its clients or about the personal affairs of your superiors to anybody outside the firm both during and after your term of employment.

If this is your understanding of the terms of our offer of employment, please complete the acceptance of employment on the accompanying copy of this letter and return the copy to us. If there is anything with which you do not agree, please feel free to discuss it with the writer.

Welcome to the firm.

Very truly yours,

_____
(signature)

Employment on the terms set out in this letter is accepted.

_____   By:_____
(date)   (signature)

FORM 401

EMPLOYMENT AGREEMENT

This employment agreement is made in two original copies between

(1)_____
            (the "Employer")

and

(2) _____
            (the "Employee")

It is agreed as follows:

1. The Employer agrees to employ the Employee and the Employee agrees to work for the Employer as a _____
            (position)

for an indefinite period of time commencing_____
                                                    (date)

2. Subject to reasonable direction by the Employer, the Employee shall perform the following duties and have the following responsibilities:

However, it is understood and agreed that these duties and responsibilities are not exhaustive and may be changed with the Employer's changing circumstances; in this regard, the Employee may not refuse any reasonable employment request by the Employer.

3. Subject to statutory holidays and ordinary vacation, the Employee shall work from _____ a.m. to _____p.m., Monday through Friday in each week of employment.

4. In addition to statutory holidays, the Employee is entitled to _____weeks' ordinary, unpaid, non-cumulative vacation in each calendar year of employment but the Employee may not take any ordinary vacation until after_____ months of employment.

5. It is understood and agreed that any ordinary vacation is subject to reasonable control over scheduling by the Employer.

FORM 402

57

6. Subject to statutory deductions, the Employer shall pay the Employee a gross cash salary, inclusive of any statutory vacation pay to which the Employee may be entitled, equivalent to _____ dollars ($ _____) per annum in weekly installments not in advance. In addition, the Employer shall make the following taxable fringe benefits available to the Employee for the term of employment:

7. The Employer shall also reimburse the Employee for all authorized business expenses incurred by the Employee in the course of employment. However, the Employee shall repay the Employer all amounts paid by the Employer to the Employee under this paragraph that are disallowed, in whole or in part, as deductible to the Employer for income tax purposes.

8. The Employee is also entitled to _____ days' paid sick leave for each complete _____ worked for the Employer.   *(time period)*

However, in order to qualify for any given period of sick leave, the Employee must provide the Employer with a doctor's certificate of the Employee's medical incapacity to work for the period claimed. It is understood and agreed that unused sick leave is lost and will not be compensated for on termination of the Employee's employment with the Employer for any reason.

9. The Employer may terminate the employment of the Employee without cause on _____ weeks' notice to the Employee. However, the Employer reserves the right to terminate the Employee's employment without notice for cause, including but not limited to death, incapacitating illness, incompetence, or failure to follow reasonable employment requests, at any time.

10. The Employee promises to keep the Employer's business secrets confidential during and after the term of employment and the Employee also promises that, on the termination of the Employee's employment with the Employer for any reason, the Employee will not operate a _____ business or in any way aid and assist any other person to operate such a business in _____ for a period of _____

_____ from the date of termination of the Employee's employment.

(time period)

11. If any provision or part of any provision in this agreement is void for any reason, it shall be severed without affecting the validity of the balance of the agreement.

FORM 402

12. Except for increases in salary or extension of employment benefits, the terms of this agreement remain in force until amended in writing signed by both parties.

13. There are no representations, warranties, conditions, terms, or collateral contracts affecting the employment contemplated in this agreement except as set out in this agreement.

14. The Employee acknowledges ample opportunity and advice to take independent legal advice in connection with the execution of this employment agreement.

15. This agreement is governed by the laws of the State of _____.

Executed under seal on_____.
                              (date)

Signed, sealed, and   )
delivered in the presence   )
of:)
)
)
_____   )   _____s
(signature of witness)   )   *(signature of employer)*
 for the Employer   )
)
_____   )   _____s
(signature of witness)   )   *(signature of employee)*
for the Employee   )

FORM 402

EMPLOYEE WARNING NOTICE

January 1, 199-

Any Company Ltd.
12 Any Street
Anytown, Anystate
12345

Dear _____

Re Employment Performance

This is to document our meeting of _____in which I drew your attention
                                                    (date)

to certain unsatisfactory aspects of your employment performance, namely,

In order to improve your performance, you must:

I will assist you in any reasonable way to meet these requirements.
However, I am giving you fair warning that, if your employment performance does not
significantly improve, I will have no option but to terminate your employment for cause.

Very truly yours,

_____
(signature)
Receipt of this warning is acknowledged.

_____   By:_____
(date)   *(signature)*

FORM 403

60

EMPLOYEE DISMISSAL LETTER

January 1, 199-

Any Company Ltd.
12 Any Street
Anytown, Anystate
12345

Dear _____

Re Termination of Employment

We regret to inform you that your employment with this firm is terminated effective on receipt of this letter for the following reason(s):

Please vacate the premises immediately with your personal possessions.
We will forward your salary earned to date in due course together with any vacation pay to which you are entitled.

Very truly yours,

_____
(signature)

FORM 404

EMPLOYEE COVENANTS: SECRECY/NON-COMPETITION

The undersigned Employee (the "Employee") of _____

_____ (the "Employer") hereby promises the Employer:

      (name of employer)

1. to keep the Employer's business secrets, including but not limited to customer, supplier, logistical, financial, research, and development information, confidential and not to disclose the Employer's business secrets to any third party during and after the term of the Employee's employment;

GENERAL NON-COMPETITION CLAUSE

2. that, on the termination of the Employee's employment with the Employer for any reason, the Employee will not operate a _____

_____ business or in any way aid and assist any other

      (type of business)

person to operate such a business in_____

      (geographical area)

for a period of _____from the date of termination of the Employee's employment;

SPECIFIC ACCOUNT NON-COMPETITION CLAUSE

3. that, on the termination of the Employee's employment with the Employer for any reason, the Employee will not solicit any customer of the Employer that was a customer of the Employer during the course of the Employee's employment with the Employer, whether or not still a customer of the Employer and whether or not knowledge of the customer is considered confidential information, or in any way aid and assist any other person to solicit any such customer for a period of _____

      (time period)

from the date of termination of the Employee's employment.

If any part of these promises is void for any reason, the undersigned accepts that it may be severed without affecting the validity or enforceability of the balance of the promises.

Given under seal on_____

      (date)

Signed, sealed, and	)	
delivered in the presence	)	
of:	)	
	)	
	)	
	)	
_____	)	_____s
(signature of witness)		*(signature of employee)*

for the Employee
FORM 405

EMPLOYEE COVENANT: EXPENSE RECOVERY

The undersigned Employee (the "Employee") of_____

_____ (the "Employer") hereby promises the Employer:
(name of employer)

To repay the Employer all amounts paid by the Employer to the Employee as compensation for or reimbursement of expenses incurred in the course of employment that are disallowed, in whole or in part, as deductible to the Employer for income tax purposes.

Given under seal on_____
                        (date)

Signed, sealed, and   )
delivered in the presence   )
of:)
)
)
_____   )   _____ s
(signature of witness)   )   *(signature of employee)*
for the Employee   )

FORM 406

63

EMPLOYEE INVENTION COVENANT

The undersigned Employee (the "Employee") of_____

_____ (the "Employer") hereby promises the Employer:
        (name of employer)

    1. to promptly disclose to the Employer in writing all inventions, discoveries, developments, innovations, and computer programs ("inventions") made, in whole or in part, by the Employee during the course of or in relation to the Employee's employment with the Employer, whether conceived or developed during working hours or not, including but not limited to inventions:

    a) resulting from work performed by the Employee or any other employee of the Employer for the Employer

    b) relating in any manner whatsoever to the present or contemplated business of the Employer, or

    c) resulting from the use of the Employer's time, equipment, materials, or work facilities;

    2. to assign and hereby does assign to the Employer all the Employee's interest in and title to inventions required to be disclosed by the Employee to the Employer;

    3. to execute at the Employer's request, whether made during or after the Employee's employment with the Employer, any instruments prepared by or on behalf of the Employer or the Employer's successors in title acknowledging or assuring the Employer's interest in and title to inventions required to be disclosed by the Employee to the Employer or assisting the Employer or the Employer's successors in title to obtain any registered copyright, design, patent, or any other industrial property rights whatsoever.

Given under seal on_____
                    (date)

Signed, sealed, and   )
delivered in the presence   )
of:)
)
)
_____) _____
(signature of witness)   ) *(signature of employee)*
for the Employee)   )

FORM 407

5
BUYING

Form 500. Invitation to quote price of goods

An offer to sell must be certain about the subject-matter and price at least before it can constitute a legally binding contract. Use this form to obtain a firm price quote.

Fill in the description of the goods you are interested in purchasing in the first line of the body of the letter.

Form 501. Demand for delivery of goods

Use this form to make formal demand for delivery of goods to set up possible repudiation of a purchase order for unreasonable delay in making delivery.

Fill in the description of the goods you ordered in the first line of the body of the letter.

Form 502. Cancellation of purchase order for late delivery

Use this form, with proper legal advice, to formally repudiate a purchase order for delay in making delivery. Note that whether delay in delivery constitutes grounds for repudiating a purchase contract depends on the delivery terms of the contract or, if nothing is said in the contract abut the importance of time of delivery, on whether the delay is implicitly unacceptable in the particular circumstance. There may be a lot of room in any particular circumstance for argument about whether the delay is unacceptable.

Fill in the description of the goods you ordered in the first line of the body of the letter.

Send a copy of this letter to your attorney and fill in name of the attorney in the last line following "copy to:."

Form 503. Rejection of non-conforming goods

Use this form to reject an entire shipment of goods that does not conform to the specifications in your purchase order.

Fill in the specific reasons for the rejection at the end of the first paragraph.

Send a copy to your attorney and fill in the name of the attorney in the last line following "copy to:."

Form 504. Partial rejection of non-conforming goods

Use this form to reject part of a shipment of goods that does not conform to the specifications in your purchase order.

Fill in specific reasons for rejection of goods at the end of the first paragraph.

Form 505. Request for instruction to return rejected goods

Use this form to request instructions from a would-be vendor on returning rejected goods.

Form 506. Conditional acceptance of non-conforming goods

Use this form where a shipment of goods does not conform to the specifications of a purchase order but you are nonetheless prepared to accept them if the vendor drops its price.

Fill in the specific reasons why the goods do not conform to your specifications at the end of the first paragraph.

Form 507. Election to return goods on approval

Use this form to return goods shipped for examination on approval.

Form 508. Conditional payment for goods reserving rights

Use this form to cover payment for a shipment of goods where you have not had a chance to properly inspect the shipment.

Form 509. Notice of defective goods

Use this form to demand unspecified satisfaction where delivered goods turn out to be defective.

Fill in the specific reasons that the goods are defective at the end of the first paragraph.

Form 510. Stop payment on check

Use this form to stop payment on your check. Your bank may require a signed specific form of its own. Telephone in the stop payment and follow it up immediately with written confirmation.

INVITATION TO QUOTE PRICE OF GOODS

January 1, 199-

Any Company Ltd.
12 Any Street
Anytown, Anystate
12345

Dear _____

Re Purchase Quote

We are interested in purchasing:

Please quote your ordinary unit price for supplying these goods together with your discount for volume purchases.

Please also indicate:

a) whether your quotes are inclusive or exclusive of sales taxes; if not otherwise stated, we will assume your quotes are inclusive of sales taxes;

b) delivery time from receipt of our purchase order to receipt of your shipment; this time frame will be a condition of any purchase order made;

c) if delivery costs are included in your quotes, your prices for pick-up at our separate cost; if delivery costs are not included in your quotes, please state this clearly otherwise we will assume they are included;

d) your terms of payment.

All price quotations must be firm and state when they expire.

Very truly yours,

_____
(signature)

FORM 500

DEMAND FOR DELIVERY OF GOODS

January 1, 199-

Any Company Ltd.
12 Any Street
Anytown, Anystate
12345

Dear _____

Re Delivery of Purchase Order

We ordered_____

_____

from you on_____ and paid for them by check dated
                            (date)

_____which has been cashed by you.

We have not yet received delivery of the goods.

Unless we receive immediate delivery of the goods, we shall cancel the order and seek the return of our money, if necessary, by legal action.

Govern yourselves accordingly.

Very truly yours,

_____
(signature)

FORM 501

CANCELLATION OF PURCHASE ORDER FOR LATE DELIVERY

January 1, 199-

Any Company Ltd.
12 Any Street
Anytown, Anystate
12345

Dear _____

Re Cancellation of Purchase Order

We ordered_____

_____

from you on_____
                          (date)

and paid for them by check dated_____ which has been cashed by you.

We demanded immediate delivery of the goods by letter dated_____.

We still have not received delivery of the goods.

We, therefore, repudiate the order for unreasonable delay in delivery and demand the return of our money.

Please be advised that, unless we receive a refund of our money in this office within 10 days of the date of this letter, we will take legal action to compel the return of our money without further notice to you.

Govern yourselves accordingly.

Very truly yours,

_____
(signature)

copy to:

FORM 502

69

REJECTION OF NON-CONFORMING GOODS

January 1, 199-

Any Company Ltd.
12 Any Street
Anytown, Anystate
12345

Dear_____

Re Rejection of Delivered Goods

We received a delivery from you further to our purchase order of_____
                                                                    (date)

but the goods delivered do not conform to the specifications of our order because of:

Accordingly, we reject the shipment and demand the return of our money.

Please be advised that, unless we receive a refund of our money in this office within 10 days of the date of this letter, we will take legal action to compel the return of our money without further notice to you.

Govern yourselves accordingly.

Also please immediately advise us as to the disposition of the rejected goods. We caution you that we will accept no responsibility for their safekeeping if we do not have your instructions as to their disposition within a reasonable time.

Very truly yours,

_____
(signature)

copy to:

FORM 503

PARTIAL REJECTION OF NON-CONFORMING GOODS

January 1, 199-

Any Company Ltd.
12 Any Street
Anytown, Anystate
12345

Dear _____

Re Partial Rejection of Delivered Goods

We received a delivery from you further to our purchase order of_____

(date)

but some of the goods delivered do not conform to the specifications of our order because of:

Accordingly, we reject these goods.

Please immediately arrange for proportionate refund of our purchase order money.

Also please immediately advise us as to the disposition of the rejected goods. We caution you that we will accept no responsibility for their safekeeping if we do not have your instructions as to their disposition within a reasonable time.

Very truly yours,

_____
(signature)

FORM 504

REQUEST FOR INSTRUCTION TO RETURN REJECTED GOODS

January 1, 199-

Any Company Ltd.
12 Any Street
Anytown, Anystate
12345

Dear_____

Re Return of Rejected Goods

Further to the rejection of the goods you delivered in purported fulfillment of our purchase
order dated_____please advise us immediately as to how you
        (date)
wish the goods disposed of.

We caution you that we will accept no responsibility for their safekeeping if we do not have
your instructions as to their disposition within a reasonable time.

Very truly yours,

_____
(signature)

FORM 505

CONDITIONAL ACCEPTANCE OF NON-CONFORMING GOODS

January 1, 199-

Any Company Ltd.
12 Any Street
Anytown, Anystate
12345

Dear_____

Re Your Delivery of Non-Conforming Goods

We received a delivery from you further to our purchase order of_____
                                                                          (date)

but the goods delivered do not conform to the specifications of our order because of:

Although the goods delivered are non-conforming, we are prepared to accept them provided you allow us a credit of $_____making the total price of our purchase order $ _____.

Please contact us immediately with regard to our proposal.

If we do not hear from you within 10 days of the date of this letter, we shall reject the shipment as non-conforming.

Very truly yours,

_____
(signature)

FORM 506

73

ELECTION TO RETURN GOODS ON APPROVAL

January 1, 199-

Any Company Ltd.
12 Any Street
Anytown, Anystate
12345

Dear_____

Re Return of Goods

Please be advised that we are electing to return the accompanying goods received from you on approval.

Very truly yours,

_____
(signature)

FORM 507

January 1, 199-
Any Company Ltd.
12 Any Street
Anytown, Anystate
12345

Dear _____

Re Conditional Payment for Goods

We have received a delivery from you further to our purchase order of_____
(date)

but have not had an opportunity of making a full and proper inspection of the shipment. Therefore, we are enclosing payment for the goods expressly reserving our rights with regard to any non-conforming found after full and proper inspection.

Very truly yours,

_____
(signature)

FORM 508

NOTICE OF DEFECTIVE GOODS

January 1, 199-

Any Company Ltd.
12 Any Street
Anytown, Anystate
12345

Dear _____

Re Notice of Defective Goods

We received a delivery from you further to our purchase order of _____
(date)

but the goods delivered are defective in that they:

Please be advised that unless we receive a satisfactory response from you within 10 days of the date of this letter, we will take legal action to enforce our rights in this unfortunate matter.

Govern yourselves accordingly.

Very truly yours,

_____

(signature)

copy to:

FORM 509

STOP PAYMENT ON CHECK

January 1, 199-

Any Company Ltd.
12 Any Street
Anytown, Anystate
12345

Dear _____

Re Check Stop Payment

Further to our telephone instructions of_____
                                              (date)
you are hereby directed to stop payment on presentation of the following check:

Account Name:

Account Number:

Check Number:

Dated:

Payable To:

Amount:

Please contact the writer for any additional information or explanation required.

Very truly yours,

_____
(signature)

FORM 510

77

6

SELLING

Form 600. Bill of sale

At a minimum, a bill of sale provides documentary proof of purchase of goods. Use this form as a template for any basic bill of sale.

Fill in a detailed list of goods following the name of the buyer at the end of the first paragraph.

Form 601. Bill of sale (without warranties)

Use this form to draft a bill of sale excluding vendor warranties. Note that it is signed by the buyer as well as the seller to underline the buyer's acceptance of the terms of sale. Many jurisdictions have "overriding" statutory vendor warranties in consumer sales.

Fill in a detailed list of goods following the name of the buyer at the end of the first paragraph.

Form 602. Bill of sale (with encumbrances)

Use this form to draft a bill of sale subject to encumbrances being assumed by the buyer (e.g., a chattel mortgage). Note that it is an agreement signed by both sides.

Fill in a detailed list of goods following the name of the Buyer at the end of the first paragraph.

Fill in the encumbrance description and encumbrance amount at the end of the second paragraph.

Form 603. Receipt for goods

Use this form to obtain the buyer's acknowledgment of receipt of goods in acceptable condition.

Fill in the name of the seller after the "To:" at the beginning of the text.

Form 604. Demand for particulars of rejection of goods

Use this form to demand the reason for rejection of a shipment of goods.

Send a copy of this letter to your attorney and fill in the name of the attorney in the last line following "copy to:."

Form 605. Refusal of rejection of goods

Use this form to reject a buyer's reasons for rejecting a shipment of goods.

Send a copy of this letter to your attorney and fill in the name of the attorney in the last line following "copy to:."

Form 606. Delivery of substituted goods

Use this form to notify a buyer of delivery of substituted goods where you are unable to fill a purchase order in exact accordance with specifications but are prepared to risk substituting other goods which you think may be acceptable.

Fill in the reasons for your inability to deliver the goods at the end of the first paragraph.

Fill in the explanation of the differences in goods sent and goods ordered at the end of the second paragraph.

Form 607. Rejected goods return instructions

Use this form to instruct a buyer how to return rejected goods. Fill in the description of the goods at the end of the first paragraph. Fill in return instructions at the end of the second paragraph.

Form 608. Replacing rejected goods

Use this form to notify a buyer who has validly rejected goods that you are replacing them.

Fill in the description of rejected goods in the first paragraph.

Fill in the instructions for return at the end of the second paragraph.

Form 609. Inability to fill purchase order

Use this form to notify a buyer that you are unable to fill a purchase order.

Fill in the reason you are unable to fill the purchase order at the end of the first paragraph.

Form 610. Late delivery of goods

Use this form to notify a buyer that delivery of goods will be delayed.

Fill in the reason for the delay at the end of the first paragraph.

Form 611. Liability exclusion clause

Exclusion or limitation clauses attempt to exclude ordinary liability for breach of contract. For obvious reasons, they are frowned on by the courts, and many jurisdictions have simply enacted legislation to override liability in non-consumer sales. Note that the exclusion or limitation is ineffective unless clearly brought to the purchaser's attention at the time of purchase.

Form 612. Limited warranty

Vendor warranties typically limit rather than add to a purchaser's legal rights (e.g., "This warranty is in place of all other warranties") and operate as exclusion clauses. Use this clause, with proper legal advice, to give a limited warranty in consumer sales. Note that the exclusion or limitation, if it can operate at all, is ineffective unless clearly brought to the purchaser's attention at the time of purchase.

BILL OF SALE

For good and valuable consideration (receipt of which is acknowledged) _____
_____ (the "Seller"),
(seller's name)

hereby sells and transfers possession of the following goods to _____
_____ (the "Buyer"):
(buyer's name)

(detailed list of goods)

The Seller warrants that it owns and has the right to sell the goods to the Buyer and that the goods are sold free and clear of all encumbrances.

Given under seal on_____
(date)

Signed, sealed, and delivered to   )
the Buyer in the presence of:)
)
_____   ) _____s
(signature of witness)   )   *(signature of seller)*

FORM 600

BILL OF SALE (WITHOUT WARRANTIES)

For good and valuable consideration (receipt of which is acknowledged_____

_____ (the "Seller") ,
(seller's name)

hereby sells and transfers possession of the following goods in their present condition and location to _____(the "Buyer"):
(buyer's name)

(detailed list of goods)

The Seller warrants that it owns and has the right to sell the goods to the Buyer and that the goods are sold free and clear of all encumbrances but makes no representations and gives no warranties as to merchantability of the goods or as to their fitness for any particular purpose or as to their safe use.

The Buyer acknowledges examining the goods and buying them "as and where is" completely at the Buyer's risk and promises not to make any claims against the Seller based upon alleged express or implied representations, warranties, or collateral agreements as to the merchantability of the goods or as to their fitness for any particular purpose or as to their safe use.

Executed in duplicate under seal on _____
(date)

Signed, sealed, and delivered to)
the Buyer in the presence of:)
)
)
_____) _____s
(signature of witness)) *(signature of seller)*
) Seller

Signed, sealed, and delivered to)
the Seller in the presence of:)
)
)
_____) _____s
(signature of witness)) *(signature of buyer)*
) Buyer

FORM 601

BILL OF SALE (WITH ENCUMBERANCES)

For good and valuable consideration (receipt of which is acknowledged) _____
_____ (the "Seller") ,
       (seller's name)

hereby sells and transfers possession of the following goods to _____
_____(the "Buyer"):
       (buyer's name)

(detailed list of goods)

The Seller warrants that it owns the goods but stipulates that they are being sold subject to the following encumbrance(s) in the following amount(s):

The Buyer acknowledges buying the goods subject to the above encumbrance(s) and promises to pay the encumbrance(s) and to indemnify and save the Seller harmless from any claim(s) based on failure to pay off the encumbrance(s).

Executed under seal in duplicate on_____
       (date)

Signed, sealed, and delivered to   )
the Buyer in the presence of:)
)
_____) _____s
(signature of witness)   ) *(signature of seller)*
) Seller

Signed, sealed, and delivered to   )
the Seller in the presence of:)
)
_____) _____s
(signature of witness)   ) *(signature of buyer)*
) Buyer

FORM 602

RECEIPT FOR GOODS

To: _____

The undersigned hereby acknowledges receipt of the goods described on the attached purchase or delivery order and that they have been inspected and found without defect in accordance with purchase order specifications.

Dated _____

_____
(signature of buyer)

FORM 603

DEMAND FOR PARTICULARS OF REJECTION OF GOODS

January 1, 199-

Any Company Ltd.
12 Any Street
Anytown, Anystate
12345

Dear _____

Re Rejection of Delivery

We delivered goods to you further to your purchase order of _____
(date)

and you rejected the shipment without adequate explanation.

Please provide us with the reasons for your rejection of the shipment forthwith.

Unless we get a satisfactory response from you within 10 days of the date of this letter, we will institute legal proceedings against you for the price of the goods without further notice.

Govern yourselves accordingly.

Very truly yours,

_____
(signature)

copy to:

FORM 604

REFUSAL OF REJECTION OF GOODS

January 1, 199-

Any Company Ltd.
12 Any Street
Anytown, Anystate
12345

Dear_____

Re Rejection of Delivery

We delivered goods to you further to your purchase order of_____
(date)

and you have rejected the shipment without lawful justification.

Unless we receive payment in full for the goods in this office within 10 days of the date of this letter, we will institute legal proceedings against you for the price of the goods without further notice.

Govern yourselves accordingly.

Very truly yours,

_____
(signature)

copy to:

FORM 605

85

DELIVERY OF SUBSTITUTED GOODS

January 1, 199-

Any Company Ltd.
12 Any Street
Anytown, Anystate
12345

Dear Customer:

Re Notice of Delivery of Substituted Goods

We are in receipt of your purchase order of_____
(date)

but, unfortunately, we are unable to deliver the specific goods you ordered at this time because of:

However, in order to accommodate your apparent needs, we are shipping substituted goods to you which only differ from the specific goods you ordered in that they:

The purchase price of the substituted goods is $_____ .

If the substituted goods are not acceptable to you, please return them at our expense by the same carrier that delivered them.

We do not expect to have the specific goods you ordered in stock until some time after

_____ .
(date)

Very truly yours,

_____
(signature)

FORM 606

REJECTED GOODS RETURN INSTRUCTIONS

January 1, 199-

Any Company Ltd.
12 Any Street
Anytown, Anystate
12345

Dear Customer:

Re Return of Rejected Goods

We acknowledge your rejection of our shipment of:

Please return the shipment to us at our cost by:

We apologize for any inconvenience this may have caused.

Very truly yours,

_____
(signature)

FORM 607

January 1, 199-

Any Company Ltd.
12 Any Street
Anytown, Anystate
12345

Dear Customer:

Re Notice of Replacing Rejected Goods

We acknowledge your rejection of:

which we shipped to you.
We are immediately shipping replacement goods to you at our cost.
Please return the rejected goods to us also at our cost by:

We apologize for any inconvenience this may have caused.

Very truly yours,

_____
(signature)

FORM 608

INABILITY TO FILL PURCHASE ORDER

January 1, 199-

Any Company Ltd.
12 Any Street
Anytown, Anystate
12345

Dear Customer:

Re Inability to Fill Purchase Order

We have received the attached purchase order but, unfortunately, are unable to fill it because of:

Accordingly, we are returning your order check.
We apologize for any inconvenience this may cause.

Very truly yours,

_____

(signature)

FORM 609

LATE DELIVERY OF GOODS

January 1, 199-

Any Company Ltd.
12 Any Street
Anytown, Anystate
12345

Dear Customer:

Re Notice of Late Delivery

We are in receipt of your purchase order of _____
                                                              (date)

but, unfortunately, are unable to deliver the goods to you at this time because of:

Please bear with us and we will fulfill your order as soon as we can.

Very truly yours,

_____
(signature)

FORM 610

90

LIABILITY EXCLUSION CLAUSE

_____
(buyer name)

acknowledges and accepts that_____
(seller name)

is not liable in contract, tort, or equity for any innocent or negligent misrepresentation made in connection with this contract or for any breach of express or implied warranty, condition, or fundamental term of this contract or for any fundamental breach of this contract or for breach of any express or implied duty of care arising in connection with this contract or for any breach of express or implied collateral contract, whether made before, at the same time, or after this contract, touching any matter affected by or affecting this contract.

FORM 611

LIMITED WARRANTY

These goods are warranted free from defects in workmanship and materials on purchase. If the goods are defective, they will be repaired or replaced, at the vendor's option, without charge on return to the vendor within_____

(period of time)

from date of purchase with satisfactory proof of purchase from the vendor and date of purchase.

This warranty is only given to the original purchaser of the goods and is void if the goods have been

— damaged by negligence or accident after purchase

— used other than for the purpose for which they are intended to be used or not used in accordance with any operating instructions supplied with the goods

— adapted or repaired other than by the vendor or an approved service center (if applicable, a list of approved service centers is available from the vendor on request), or

— added on to or used with other goods which may affect the integrity, performance, safety, or reliability of these goods.

This warranty is given in place of all other warranties and assurances, whether express or implied, including but not limited to matters of quality, fitness for purpose, or merchantability and the vendor accepts no liability, under any circumstances whatsoever, for any consequential damage or loss suffered by anyone as a result of using or being unable to use the goods.

Certain jurisdictions have consumer protection laws which give you additional rights.

FORM 612

7
COLLECTIONS

a. SELLER'S FORMS

Form 700. Request for payment

Use this form to request payment of your account.

Form 701. Second request for payment

Use this form to make a second request for payment of your account.

Form 702. Final demand for payment

Use this form to make a final demand for payment of your account prior to instituting collection proceedings.

Form 703. Bad check letter

Use this form to notify a payer of a returned check.

Form 704. Installment payment agreement

Use this form to document an agreement to pay off a debt with interest in monthly installments.

Form 705. Receipt for payment

Use this form to draft a receipt for payment.

Form 706. Collection instructions to attorney

Use this form to instruct your attorney to commence collection proceedings.

Insert a description of the debt in the first paragraph following the full address of the debtor.

Select among the relevant documents by underlining, circling, or highlighting the pertinent ones.

b. BUYER'S FORMS

Form 707. Notice of disputed account

Use this form to notify an alleged creditor that you dispute the creditor's account.

Insert description of account in first paragraph.

Choose the reason for disputing the balance by underlining, circling, or highlighting the correct one.

Form 708. Settlement offer of disputed account

Use this form to make an offer to settle a demand for payment of a disputed account.

Form 709. Agreement to compromise disputed account

Use this form to draft a formal agreement with a vendor to accept a lesser payment on a disputed account.

January 1, 199-

Any Company
12 Any Street
Anytown, Anystate
12345

Dear _____

Re Payment of Account

Further to our invoice dated _____ in the amount of $_____
                                                    (date)

we have not yet received payment.

We are sure that this is merely an oversight and would ask you to send the payment now.

Very truly yours,

_____
(signature)

FORM 700

SECOND REQUEST FOR PAYMENT

January 1, 199-

Any Company
12 Any Street
Anytown, Anystate
12345

Dear_____

Re Second Request for Payment

Further to our invoice dated _____ in the amount of $ _____
                                                    (date)

and our request for payment of _____ we still have not received payment.
                                                (date)

Again we would ask you to send the payment now.

Very truly yours,

_____
(signature)

FORM 701

FINAL DEMAND FOR PAYMENT

January 1, 199-

Any Company
12 Any Street
Anytown, Anystate
12345

Dear _____

Re Final Demand for Payment

Further to our invoice dated _____ in the amount of $_____,
                                    (date)

we have not yet received payment.

Please be advised that unless we receive payment in full of our invoice in this office within 10 days of the date of this letter, we will institute collection proceedings without further notice to you.

These proceedings will include claims for pre-judgment interest and legal costs and will substantially increase the amount owing by you to us.

Govern yourselves accordingly.

Very truly yours,

_____
(signature)

FORM 702

96

BAD CHECK LETTER

January 1, 199-

Any Company
12 Any Street
Anytown, Anystate
12345

Dear _____

Re Bad check

Please be advised that your check to us dated _____has been returned because of insufficient funds.

This is a serious matter and we would ask you to replace the check immediately.

Unless we have a replacement check in this office within 10 days of the date of this letter, we will institute collection proceedings without further notice to you.

These proceedings will include claims for pre-judgment interest and legal costs and will substantially increase the amount owing by you to us.

Govern yourselves accordingly.

Very truly yours,

_____
(signature)

FORM 703

INSTALLMENT PAYMENT AGREEMENT

January 1, 199-

Any Company
12 Any Street
Anytown, Anystate
12345

Dear _____

Re Installment Payment Arrangement

This is to confirm the arrangement under which we will accept payment of our outstanding account of $_____ in installments.

You will sign and return the enclosed copy of this letter indicating admission of the full amount of the account and acceptance of the terms of our agreement.

We will then accept payment of the account, together with interest at the rate of _____% per annum, compounded annually, in consecutive, monthly installments of $_____commencing_____ and continuing on the
                                                    (date)

_____ of each successive month until paid off in full. Time will be
      (day)

considered to be of the essence of this arrangement. Each payment will be applied, first, to accrued interest and, second, to principal.

If there is default in making any payment, at our option the full balance owing on the account, together with accrued agreed interest, shall immediately become due and payable and continue to accrue interest, before and after judgment at the same rate of interest until paid off in full.

Please return the signed copy of this agreement with your first payment before the commencement date of the monthly installments; otherwise this agreement is null and void.

Very truly yours,

_____
(signature)

FORM 704

Admission and Acceptance

The undersigned hereby admits the full amount of the above outstanding account and having no rights of set-off or counterclaim and accepts the above terms of payment.

Dated _____19_____   _____
                                                        (signature)

FORM 704

RECEIPT FOR PAYMENT

_____ 19_____

RECEIVED FROM _____

_____ DOLLARS

$_____ FOR _____

_____

_____
(signature)

FORM 705

COLLECTION INSTRUCTIONS TO ATTORNEYS

January 1, 199-

Any Company
12 Any Street
Anytown, Anystate
12345

Dear _____

Re Institution of Collection Proceedings

Please accept this letter as your instructions to immediately commence collection proceedings on our behalf against_____
(full name of debtor)

of _____
(full address of debtor)

for _____
(describe debt)

in the amount of $_____.

We enclose copies of the relevant documents:

    — purchase order

    — invoice

    — bad check and notice of return

    — correspondence

for your file. We shall keep the original documents safe for production in court as necessary.

If you need further documents or information, please contact the writer.

We would ask you to keep us informed of the progress of this matter and to consult us when our legal bill reaches $ _____ .

Very truly yours,

_____
(signature)
Encs.

FORM 706

NOTICE OF DISPUTED ACCOUNT

January 1, 199-

Any Company
12 Any Street
Anytown, Anystate
12345

Dear _____

Re Disputed Account

We acknowledge receipt of your statement of account for _____

_____
(describe)

dated_____ .

We dispute the balance indicated as owing by us on the ground that no goods were ordered by us [OR] no goods have been received by us [OR] the goods delivered do not meet the specifications set out in our purchase order [OR] some of the goods delivered do not meet the specifications set out in our purchase order [OR] the goods delivered are defective [OR] some of the goods delivered are defective [OR] we have paid the amount in question [OR] the amount is incorrect because:

Please contact the writer immediately to discuss the adjustment of our account.

Very truly yours,

_____
(signature)

FORM 707

SETTLEMENT OFFER OF DISPUTED ACCOUNT

January 1, 199-

Any Company
12 Any Street
Anytown, Anystate
12345

Dear _____

Re Disputed Account

This is in connection with the demand for payment of your invoice dated_____

As you know, we dispute the balance indicated as owing by us.

Without admitting liability and solely for the purpose of a quick resolution of this unfortunate matter, we are prepared to offer an immediate payment of $ _____ in full settlement of your disputed account.

If this proposal is acceptable to you, please advise us in writing and we will send the payment by return mail.

Very truly yours,

_____
(signature)

FORM 708

AGREEMENT TO COMPROMISE DISPUTED ACCOUNT

Whereas _____ (the "Claimant")
                            (claimant's name)

has a claim against _____(the "Disputant")
                                (disputant's name)

on a disputed invoice dated _____ in the amount

of $_____.

It is agreed as follows:

1. The Claimant will accept a lesser payment of $ _____ in full settlement of its claim on the invoice.

2. If the Disputant does not pay the lesser payment in full to the Claimant within_____ days of receipt back of an original copy of this agreement executed by both parties, the Claimant may sue the Disputant for the full amount of its disputed invoice.

3. If the Claimant's claim on its disputed invoice is compromised pursuant to this agreement, the parties mutually release each other from any and all claims and rights of action against each other, present and future, arising in connection with their dispute over payment of the disputed invoice.

4. This agreement binds and benefits the parties and their respective heirs, executors, administrators, personal representatives, successors, and assigns.

Executed under seal in duplicate on _____.
                                                    (date)

Signed, sealed, and   )
delivered in the presence   )
of:)
)
)
_____   ) _____s
(signature of witness)   ) *(signature of disputant)*
for the Disputant   ) The Disputant
)
_____   ) _____s
(signature of witness)   ) *(signature of claimant)*
for the Claimant   ) The Claimant

FORM 709

104

8
CREDIT/DEBIT

Form 800. Personal credit application

Use this form to obtain credit information. Be careful about disclosing credit information obtained from a customer to third parties — the information was probably given in confidence and there may be laws regulating its disclosure.

Insert name of your firm at the end of the section titled, "Certificate."

Form 801. Authority to release credit information

Use this form to obtain the customer's authority to disclose and release credit information from a specific source to your firm. The disclosure of credit-related information about a customer may be regulated by law.

Form 802. Demand promissory note

Promissory notes are special promises to pay which can be endorsed over to someone else like checks. They are frequently used as simple documentary evidence of indebtedness. Use this form to draw up a simple promissory note payable on demand.

Form 803. Joint and several demand promissory note

Use this form to draw up a simple promissory note payable by more than one person on demand.

Form 804. Due date promissory note

Use this form to draw up a simple promissory note payable on a specified future date.

Form 805. Series form promissory note

Use this form to draw up a series of installment payment promissory notes.

Form 806. Periodic payment promissory note

Use this form to draw up a single promissory note providing for installment payments.

Form 807. Demand for payment on demand promissory note

A demand promissory note requires a demand for payment to make it due and payable. Use this form to make demand for payment on a demand promissory note. Note that "payable on demand" means "payable within a reasonably prompt time after demand," which depends on the circumstances.

Form 808. Payment in full demand on installment promissory note

Use this form to make demand for accelerated payment in full of an installment promissory note which provides for the whole balance becoming due on default in making an installment payment.

Send a copy of this letter to your attorney. Insert your attorney's name following "copy to:."

Form 809. Installment payment demand on promissory note

Use this form to make demand for payment of an overdue installment under an installment promissory note which provides for the whole balance becoming due on default in making an installment payment. The next step is demanding payment of the whole balance.

Form 810. Guarantee
Use this form to draft a guarantee of payment by a third party.

Form 811. Demand for payment on guarantee
Use this form to demand payment on a guarantee.

Send a copy of this letter to your attorney. Insert your attorney's name following "copy to:."

PERSONAL CREDIT APPLICATION

Full name of applicant: _____

Present address: _____

_____

Home phone: (   ) _____ Work phone: (   ) _____

HOME:

Do you rent or own your present address?   (   ) rent   (   ) own

How many years have you lived at your present address?

Previous address(es):

_____

from _____ to _____

_____

from _____ to _____

_____

from _____ to _____

WORK:

Are you employed or in business?   (   ) employed   (   ) in business

IF EMPLOYED:

What is your present employment? _____

Name of your present employer? _____

Present employer's address? _____

_____

How many years have you worked for your present employer? _____

IF IN BUSINESS:

What type of business are you in? _____

Name of business? _____

Address of business? _____

_____

How many years have you owned this business? _____

FORM 800

107

IF EMPLOYED OR OWNED BUSINESS LESS THAN TWO YEARS:

Previous employment _____

Name of previous employer _____

Previous employer's address _____

_____

How many years did you work for your previous employer? _____

ANNUAL INCOME:

Gross base income from employment	$_____
Gross overtime income	$_____
Gross income from commissions	$_____
Net income from business	$_____
Net rental income	$_____
Dividend/interest income	$_____
Other income (specify):	$_____
	$_____
Total annual income	$_____

ASSETS (estimate value):		DEBTS (estimate amount):	
Home	$_____	Mortgage	$_____
Car	$_____	Car loan	$_____
Savings/Bonds	$_____	Bank loan	$_____
_____	$_____	Credit cards	$_____
_____	$_____	_____	$_____
_____	$_____	_____	$_____
_____	$_____	_____	$_____
_____	$_____	_____	$_____
_____	$_____	_____	$_____
Total assets	$_____	Total debts:	$_____

BANKRUPTCY: Have you gone bankrupt in the last five years? ( ) yes ( ) no

If yes, give date of assignment: _____

CERTIFICATE: I certify the above information to be accurate and complete and hereby authorize the disclosure and release of any credit-related information about myself to

_____
(firm name)

Dated: _____   Signed:_____

FORM 800

AUTHORITY TO RELEASE CREDIT INFORMATION

To: _____

(information holder)

From: _____

(credit applicant)

The undersigned hereby authorizes the disclosure and release of any and all personal credit-related information in your possession, including but not limited to credit, financial, salary, banking, debt, and tax information and materials, to_____

_____

(your firm name)

as required, until further notice.

Dated:_____.

_____   _____

(signature of witness)   *(signature of applicant)*

Witness   Credit Applicant

FORM 801

DEMAND PROMISSORY NOTE

$_____

For value received, the undersigned promises to pay _____
                                                                        (payee)
or order on demand the sum of _____
dollars, together with interest from this date at the rate of _____% per annum,
both before and after default, until paid in full.

Signed at _____on_____

_____   _____
(signature of witness)   *(signature of promissor)*
Witness

FORM 802

JOINT AND SEVERAL DEMAND PROMISSORY NOTE

$_____

For value received, the undersigned, jointly and severally promise to pay_____

_____
         (payee)

or order on demand the sum of _____dollars, together with interest
from this date at the rate of _____% per annum, both before and after default,
until paid in full.

Signed at_____on_____

_____   _____
(signature of witness)   *(signature of promissor 1)*
Witness

_____   _____
(signature of witness)   *(signature of promissor 2)*
Witness

DUE DATE PROMISSORY NOTE

$_____

For value received, the undersigned promises to pay _____
(payee)

or order on or before_____ the sum of _____
(date)

dollars, together with interest from this date at the rate _____% per annum
both before and after default, until paid in full.

Signed at_____ on_____

_____   _____
(signature of witness)   (signature of promissor)

Witness

FORM 804

SERIES FORM PROMISSORY NOTE

$_____

For value received, the undersigned promises to pay_____
                                                                                          (payee)

or order on or before _____the sum of _____
                                           (date)

dollars, together with interest from this date at the rate of_____% per annum, both before and after default, until paid in full.

This note is No_____in a series of _____notes given by

_____
                                           (debtor)

to secure payment of a principal debt in the total amount of _____dollars
($ _____).

If there is a default in the payment of this note, at the option of its holder, any remaining notes in the series also held by the holder, shall immediately become due and payable.

Signed at _____on_____

_____   _____
(signature of witness)   *(signature of promissor)*
Witness

PERIODIC PAYMENT PROMISSORY NOTE

$_____

For value received, the undersigned promises to pay_____
(payee)

or order the principal sum of _____ dollars, together with interest from
this date at the rate of_____% per annum, both before and after default, until
paid in full, in monthly installments of _____dollars ($_____),
commencing_____and on the _____day of
each successive month, until _____when any unpaid principal
and accrued interest on the note shall become due and payable.

This note may be prepaid in whole or in part at any time without penalty.

All payments on this note shall be made at _____

_____
(address)

during normal business hours or at such other reasonable place as the holder may designate
in writing from time to time.

All payments and prepayments made on this note shall be applied first to accrued interest
and then to principal.

If there is a default in making the monthly payments on this note, at the option of its holder,
its unpaid principal and accrued interest shall immediately become due and payable.

For value received, if there is a default in making any payment on this note, the undersigned
also promises to pay_____
(payee)

on demand all reasonably incurred costs of enforcing payment on the note, including, but
not necessarily limited to, legal costs.

The undersigned waives presentation for payment, notice of non-payment, protest, and
notice of protest in connection with this note.

Signed at _____on_____

_____   _____
(signature of witness)   *(signature of promissor)*

Witness

FORM 806

114

DEMAND FOR PAYMENT ON DEMAND PROMISSORY NOTE

January 1, 199-

12 Any Street
Anytown, Anystate
12345

Dear _____

Re Demand for Payment on Note

I am the holder of your promissory note dated _____in the amount
of $ _____payable to_____
(payee)

or order on demand.

I am making formal demand for payment by you at _____

_____
(address)

of the full, unpaid balance of the note, together with all accrued and accruing interest,
within a reasonable time of receipt of this letter.

Please be advised that a reasonable time for payment on a demand note is relatively short.

Very truly yours,

_____
(signature)

FORM 807

115

PAYMENT IN FULL DEMAND ON INSTALLMENT PROMISSORY NOTE

January 1, 199-

12 Any Street
Anytown, Anystate
12345

Dear_____

Re Demand for Payment on Note

I am the holder of your promissory note dated_____ in the amount of $ _____ payable to _____ or order.
                            (payee)

You are in default on the note for failure to pay the installment due on _____
                                                                      (date)

in the amount of $_____ .

I am, therefore, demanding immediate payment of the full, unpaid balance of the note together with all accrued and accruing interest.

Unless I receive payment of the note in full in this office within 10 days of the date of this letter, I will take legal action to enforce payment without further notice to you.

Govern yourself accordingly.

Very truly yours,

_____
(signature)

copy to:

FORM 808

116

INSTALLMENT PAYMENT DEMAND ON PROMISSORY NOTE

January 1, 199-

12 Any Street
Anytown, Anystate
12345

Dear_____

Re Demand for Installment Payment on Note

I am the holder of your installment promissory note dated_____

in the amount of $_____payable to _____

(payee)

or order.

You are in default on the note for failure to pay the installment due on _____

in the amount of $_____.

Unless I receive payment of the installment in full in this office within 10 days of the date of this letter, I will demand immediate payment of the remaining balance of the note.

Govern yourself accordingly.

Very truly yours,

_____

(signature)

FORM 809

GUARANTEE

In consideration of _____
_____(the "Creditor")

accepting the payment promise of _____
_____(the "Debtor")

the undersigned _____
_____(the "Guarantor")

hereby unconditionally guarantees the Creditor prompt and full payment of all amounts which are now or may become owing by the Debtor to the Creditor.

The obligation of the Guarantor under this guarantee is limited to a maximum amount of _____ dollars ($ _____).

This guarantee is intended to operate notwithstanding any renewals, extensions, or indulgences of any kind granted the Debtor by the Creditor, or the release or change of any security given by the Debtor to the Creditor to secure the Debtor's payment promise ("Security"), or any failure or neglect on the part of the Creditor to enforce payment by the Debtor or to protect any Security, and the Creditor may call upon the guarantee as a first, principal obligation without previously demanding payment from the Debtor or any co-guarantor or realizing any Security.

This guarantee is also intended to operate as a continuing, absolute obligation and remains in force until revoked by notice in writing from the Guarantor to the Creditor, which revocation shall not affect the guarantee of prompt and full payment of any amount owed by the Debtor to the Creditor as of the date of actual receipt of notice of revocation by the Creditor.

If more than one person executes this guarantee, their obligation under this guarantee is joint and several.

Given under seal on _____.
_____(date)

Signed, sealed, and   )
delivered in the presence   )
of:)
)
)
_____   )   _____s
(signature of witness)   )
for   )
)
)
_____   )   _____s
(signature of witness)   )
for   )

FORM 810

118

DEMAND FOR PAYMENT ON GUARANTEE

January 1, 199-

Any Company
12 Any Street
Anytown, Anystate
12345

Dear_____

Re Demand for Payment on Guarantee

We hold your guarantee dated _____ for the indebtedness to us of

_____
      (Debtor)

This is to advise you that the indebtedness has reached the amount of $ _____,
including interest, as set out in the enclosed statement of account.

Please be advised that unless we receive payment of the indebtedness in this office within
10 days of the date of this letter, we will institute collection proceedings against the debtor
and you without further notice.

Govern yourself accordingly.

Very truly yours,

_____
(signature)

copy to:

FORM 811

119

9
LEASES

Form 900. Commercial lease

Use this form with proper legal advice, to draft a lease of commercial premises. Do not use this form for residential premises because many jurisdictions have special legislation governing and protecting residential tenancies.

In section 4(b), for "additional rent," insert items such as landlord's business taxes, property taxes, school taxes, repairs to building, heating, water rates, electric rates, maintenance costs, building security, management fees, and landlord's fire and public liability insurance premiums.

In section 5, insert as sole responsibility and expense of the Tenant items such as tenant's business taxes, repairs to premises, utilities separately metered, leasehold improvements, and janitorial services.

In section 6, insert as sole responsibility and expense of the landlord items such as landlord's business taxes, property taxes, school taxes, repairs to building, heating, water rates, electric rates, maintenance costs, building security, management fees, and landlord's fire and public liability insurance premiums.

Form 901. Exercising option to renew lease

Use this form to exercise an option to renew a lease.

Form 902. Notice of rent default

Use this form to demand payment of arrears of rent under a commercial lease.

Form 903. Notice of other lease default

Use this form to demand remedy of default under a commercial lease other than in connection with payment of rent.

Insert specifics of breach of lease at end of first paragraph.

Form 904. Landlord notice of termination of lease

Use this form to give landlord's notice of terminating a commercial lease. Note that this is appropriate both on expiration of a fixed lease term to prevent the tenant overholding "with consent" and, with proper legal advice, to terminate an informal, periodic (e.g. month-to-month) lease.

Form 905. Tenant notice of termination of lease

Use this form to give tenant's notice of quitting a commercial lease.

Form 906. Agreement to cancel lease

Use this form to draft an agreement to cancel a lease.

Form 907. Assignment of lease

Use this form to draft an assignment of lease. Note the involvement of the landlord in the assignment because most leases are expressed to be non-assignable without the landlord's consent.

Form 908. Amendment of lease

Use this form, preferably with proper legal advice, to draft commercial lease amendments.

Insert particulars of amendment at the end of the third paragraph following "as follows."

Form 909. Commercial sublease

Use this form, preferably with proper legal advice, to draft a sublease of commercial premises.

COMMERCIAL LEASE

This lease is made in duplicate between:

(1)_____(the "Landlord")
　　　　　(landlord name)

and

(2)_____(the "Tenant")
　　　　　(tenant name)

The Landlord and the Tenant hereby agree as follows:

1.　　The Landlord hereby grants the Tenant a lease of the premises outlined in red on the floor plan attached as Schedule A located on the_____floor of

_____
　　　　　　　　　　　　　　　　(address)

_____ (the "Premises.")

The parties agree that the Premises have a rented area of_____ square feet, excluding the exterior walls.

2.　　The term of this lease commences on_____and ends on _____. If the Tenant continues in occupation of the Premises with the consent of the Landlord after expiry of the term of this lease, the Tenant shall be deemed to be leasing the Premises on a month-to-month basis but otherwise on the same terms as set out in this lease.

3.　　The Tenant may use the Premises for_____
　　　　　　　　　　　　　　　　　　　(business purpose)

and for no other purpose.

4.　　(a)　The Tenant shall pay the Landlord a "base rent" of_____dollars
　　　　　　($ _____)per year in equal monthly installments of_____

　　　　　　_____dollars ($_____) in advance on or before the first of each month commencing on _____with the base rent for any broken portion of a calendar month in which this lease terminates being prorated.

　　　　(b)　The following services and expenses are the responsibility of the Landlord, _____% of the total cost of which services and expenses during the term of this lease shall be paid by the Tenant to the Landlord as "additional rent":

FORM 900

121

(c) The Landlord shall invoice the Tenant monthly for additional rent incurred during the preceding calendar month. Each invoice is payable in full thirty days after delivery. The Tenant is deemed to have admitted the accuracy of the amount charged in any invoice for additional rent which he or she has not challenged in writing within the same thirty days.

(d) The Tenant shall also pay the Landlord as "additional rent", on demand, 100% of the total costs reasonably incurred by the Landlord, including but not limited to legal fees, of curing any default of the Tenant under this lease, including but not limited to enforcing payment of rent and regaining lawful possession of the Premises.

5.   The following services and expenses are the sole responsibility and expense of the Tenant:

6.   The following services and expenses are the sole responsibility and expense of the Landlord:

7.   The Landlord shall also be solely responsible for repairs or improvements to the structure and to the exterior of the building.

8.   Any services and expenses relevant to the use by the Tenant of the Premises and not mentioned in this lease are the responsibility and expense of the Tenant.

9.   The Landlord covenants with the Tenant that so long as the Tenant complies with the terms of this lease, the Tenant may occupy and enjoy the Premises without any interruption from the Landlord.

FORM 900

10. The Landlord is not liable for any damage to the Tenant's property or for any injury to any person in or coming to or from the Premises, however caused, and the Tenant agrees to indemnify the Landlord against the financial consequences of any such liability. In this regard, the Tenant shall purchase and maintain public liability insurance in the amount of no less than _____ dollars ($ _____) and shall provide proof of this insurance to the Landlord on request.

11. The Landlord may terminate this lease for any one of the following or any other cause permitted by law:

(a) fifteen days' arrears of rent or additional rent;

(b) the bankruptcy or insolvency of the Tenant;

(c) a material change in the use of the Premises by the Tenant, and in particular (without limiting the generality of this provision) any change which affects the Landlord's building insurance or which constitutes a nuisance.

(d) any unauthorized assignment or subletting of this lease by the Tenant;

(e) substantial damage to or destruction of the Premises;

(f) any sale or material change in use of the building in which the Premises are located by the Landlord;

(g) any significant wilful or negligent damage to the Premises caused by the Tenant or by persons permitted on the Premises by the Tenant.

12. The Tenant may not assign or sublet the Premises, in whole or in part, or allow the Premises to be used by any other person without the written consent of the Landlord, which consent_____ be unreasonably withheld.

13. The Tenant shall keep the Premises in a reasonable state of repair and cleanliness and shall not make improvements or alterations to the Premises without the written consent of the Landlord, which consent shall not be unreasonably withheld.

14. At the end of the lease, the Tenant shall deliver vacant possession to the Landlord of the Premises in the same condition as at the commencement of the lease, reasonable wear and tear excepted and except that the Landlord may, in the Landlord's sole discretion, elect to keep any of the Tenant's improvements, alterations, or fixtures.

15. Any written notice required or permitted to be given by this lease is sufficiently given if sent in proper form by ordinary mail to the last known address of the party for whom the notice is intended. Any written notice sent by ordinary mail in accordance with this paragraph is deemed, for the purposes of this lease, received by the addressee on the seventh day after mailing unless actually received before. Nothing in this paragraph prevents giving written notice in any other manner recognized by law.

16. In this lease, words importing the singular include the plural, and vice versa, and importing the masculine gender include the feminine, and importing an individual include a corporation and vice versa. This lease binds and benefits the parties and their respective heirs, successors, and permitted assigns.

FORM 900

17.   If not in default under this lease, the Tenant has the right to renew this lease for a further term of _____ years exercisable by giving written notice of renewal to the Landlord in the six-month period immediately before the expiry of the original fixed term of this lease. The renewed lease is granted on the same terms as set out in this lease except as to base rent and without any further right of renewal. The base rent payable by the Tenant in the renewed term may be agreed between the Landlord and Tenant but, failing such agreement before commencement of the renewed term of the lease, the amount of the base rent shall be settled by arbitration in accordance with the rules of the American Arbitration Association in force at that time and judgment on the arbitration award may be entered in any court of competent jurisdiction.

Executed under seal on _____.
                              (date)

Signed, sealed, and   )
delivered in the presence   )
of:)
)
)
_____   ) _____s
(signature of witness)   ) *(signature of landlord)*
for the Landlord   ) The Landlord
)
)
_____   ) _____s
(signature of witness)   ) *(signature of tenant)*
for the Tenant   ) The Tenant

FORM 900

EXERCISING OPTION TO RENEW LEASE

January 1, 199-

Any Company
12 Any Street
Anytown, Anystate
12345

Dear _____

Re Renewal of Lease

This is to notify you that we are exercising the option to renew our lease of _____
_____
       (address)

for a further term of_____ years contained in _____
                                                  (section reference)

of the lease.

   [IF ARBITRATED RENT]

Please advise us of the rent you propose to charge in the renewed term so that we can decide whether or not to submit the matter to arbitration in accordance with the provisions of _____of the lease.

(section reference)

Very truly yours,

_____

(signature)

FORM 901

125

NOTICE OF RENT DEFAULT

January 1, 199-

Any Company
12 Any Street
Anytown, Anystate
12345

Dear _____

Re Rent Arrears

You are presently in arrears of rent in the amount of $_____ in connection
with your lease of _____.
                                                    (address)

Please remedy this situation within 10 days of the date of this letter or we will terminate
the lease and institute collection proceedings without further notice to you.

Very truly yours,

_____
(signature)

FORM 902

NOTICE OF OTHER LEASE DEFAULT

January 1, 199-

Any Company
12 Any Street
Anytown, Anystate
12345

Dear _____

Re Lease Default

You are presently in breach of _____ of your lease of _____
                                    (section reference)

_____
            (address)

by reason of _____

_____

_____

_____

_____

_____

Please remedy this situation within a reasonable time or we will terminate the lease.

Very truly yours,

_____
(signature)

FORM 903

LANDLORD NOTICE OF TERMINATION OF LEASE

January 1, 199-

Any Company
12 Any Street
Anytown, Anystate
12345

Dear _____

Re Notice of Termination of Lease

This is to notify you to quit and deliver up possession of _____

_____
      (address)

you presently occupy as our tenant, by _____.
                                                      (date)

We remind you of your obligation to leave the premises in a reasonable condition at the end of your tenancy.

Very truly yours,

_____
(signature)

FORM 904

TENANT NOTICE OF TERMINATION OF LEASE

January 1, 199-

Any Company
12 Any Street
Anytown, Anystate
12345

Dear_____

Re Notice of Termination of Lease

This is to notify you of our intention to quit and deliver up possession of _____
_____
      (address)

which we presently occupy as your tenant, on _____
                                                     (date)

Very truly yours,

_____
(signature)

AGREEMENT TO CANCEL LEASE

Whereas

_____ (the "Landlord")
                    (landlord name)

and

_____ (the "Tenant")
                    (tenant name)

executed a lease dated _____(the "Lease") of certain premises located at

_____ the ("Premises")
                    (address)

but the parties now wish to cancel the Lease;

It is agreed as follows:

1. In return for the Tenant vacating the Premises on or before _____,
                                                            (the "Termination Date")

the Lease is cancelled effective that date and the parties will have no further obligation to each other under the Lease.

2. Nothing in this agreement operates to discharge obligations and liabilities accrued under the Lease up to the date of its cancellation.

3. If the Tenant does not vacate the Premises on or before the Termination Date, this agreement is null and void.

4. This agreement binds and benefits the parties and their respective heirs, executors, administrators, personal representatives, successors, and assigns.

Executed in duplicate under seal on _____.
                                              (date)

Signed, sealed, and   )
delivered in the presence   )
of:)
)
)
_____   ) _____s
(signature of witness)   )   (signature of landlord)
for the Landlord   )   The Landlord
)
)
_____   ) _____s
(signature of witness)   )   (signature of tenant)
for the Tenant   )   the Tenant

FORM 906

ASSIGNMENT OF LEASE

Whereas

_____ (the "Landlord")
       (landlord name)

and

_____ (the "Present Tenant")
       (present tenant name)

have entered into the lease appended as Schedule A to this assignment (the "Lease");

And whereas the Present Tenant wishes to assign its rights and interest in the Lease to

_____ the "Proposed Tenant"
       (proposed tenant name)

and the Landlord consents to the assignment;

It is agreed as follows:

1. The Present Tenant hereby assigns all its rights and interest in the Lease to the Proposed Tenant.

2. The Landlord hereby consents to the assignment.

3. The Proposed Tenant covenants with the Landlord and the Present Tenant to observe and perform all the terms of the Lease.

[TO RELEASE PRESENT TENANT'S LIABILITY]

4. The Landlord hereby releases the Present Tenant from all further liability under the Lease but nothing in this assignment operates to discharge obligations and liabilities accrued under the Lease up to the date of this assignment.

[OR]

[TO RETAIN PRESENT TENANT'S LIABILITY]

4. Nothing in this assignment operates to release the Present Tenant from its obligations and liabilities under the Lease.

FORM 907

5. This assignment binds and benefits the parties and their respective heirs, executors, administrators, personal representatives, successors and assigns.

Executed in triplicate under seal on _____.

(date)

Signed, sealed, and   )
delivered in the presence   )
of:)
)

_____) _____s

(signature of witness)   ) *(signature of present tenant)*

for the Present Tenant   ) The Present Tenant
)

_____) _____s

(signature of witness)   ) *(signature of proposed tenant)*

for the Proposed Tenant   ) The Proposed Tenant
)

_____) _____s

(signature of witness)   ) *(signature of landlord)*

for the Landlord   ) The Landlord

FORM 907

AMENDMENT OF LEASE

Whereas

_____ (the "Landlord")
            (landlord name)

and

_____ (the "Tenant")
            (tenant name)

have entered into the lease of which a copy is appended as Schedule A to this agreement (the "Lease");

And whereas the Landlord and the Tenant wish to amend the terms of the Lease;

The parties agree to amend the Lease as follows:

All other terms of the Lease remain as stated.

Executed in duplicate under seal on _____.
                                              (date)

Signed, sealed, and   )
delivered in the presence   )
of:)
)
_____   )   _____s
(signature of witness)   )   *(signature of tenant)*
for the Tenant   )   The Tenant
)
_____   )   _____s
(signature of witness)   )   *(signature of landlord)*
for the Landlord   )   The Landlord

FORM 908

COMMERCIAL SUBLEASE

This sublease is made between:

(1)_____ (the "Sublandlord")
         (sublandlord name)

and

(2) _____ (the "Subtenant").
         (subtenant name)

Whereas

_____(the "Landlord")
         (landlord name)

and the Sublandlord have entered into a lease of premises (the "Premises") of which a copy is appended as Schedule A to this agreement (the "Lease");

And whereas the Sublandlord and the Subtenant wish to enter into a sublease of the Premises for the balance of the term of the Lease less one day;

And whereas the Landlord has consented to this sublease;

The Sublandlord and Subtenant agree as follows:

1. The Sublandlord hereby subleases the Premises to the Subtenant to have and to hold for the balance of the term of the Lease less one day commencing on _____ .

The Subtenant, however, may not assign or sublease its interest in the Premises without the consent of the Sublandlord, which consent expressly may be unreasonably withheld.

2. The Subtenant shall pay rent of_____ dollars ($_____) per month in advance on the first day of each and every month during the term of this sublease with the rent for any broken portion of a calendar month in which this sublease terminates being prorated.

3. The Subtenant agrees to pay to the Sublandlord all sums which the Sublandlord is required to pay to the Landlord under the Lease as additional rent pursuant to the provisions of the Lease or is required to pay to the Landlord by reason of the Subtenant's occupancy of the Premises.

4. The Subtenant agrees to observe and perform all the Sublandlord's covenants in the Lease apart from the payment of rent and additional rent to the Landlord.

5. The Subtenant shall pay all business taxes in respect of the business carried on by the Subtenant in and upon or by reason of its occupancy of the Premises.

6. The Subtenant shall take out and keep in force during the term of the sublease such insurance in respect of the Premises as to comply with the obligations of the Sublandlord under the Lease and shall be subject, as regards both the Landlord and the Sublandlord, to the same obligations and same limitations of liability with respect to damage, loss, or injury as are set out in the Lease between the Landlord and the Sublandlord.

FORM 909

7. The Sublandlord covenants with the Subtenant:

    a) for quiet enjoyment of the Premises;

    b) to pay all rent and additional rent reserved under the Lease;

    c) to enforce for the benefit of the Subtenant of the Premises the obligations of the Landlord under the Lease with the intent that the benefit of such covenants extend to the Premises to be enjoyed by the Subtenant; the Subtenant, however, agrees to pay the Sublandlord's costs, including but not limited to legal costs, reasonably incurred by the Sublandlord in relation to such enforcement.

8. The rights and obligations of the Subtenant with respect to the installation, alteration or removal of fixtures and improvements and signs shall be governed by the applicable provisions of the Lease.

9. The provisions of the Lease regarding the Landlord's remedies against the Sublandlord and the Premises in connection with the Sublandlord's default under the Lease are hereby incorporated in this sublease for the benefit of the Sublandlord against the Subtenant and the Premises in connection with the Subtenant's default under this sublease.

Executed in duplicate under seal on_____.

                              (date)

Signed, sealed, and   )

delivered in the presence   )

of:)

)

_____) _____s

(signature of witness)   ) *(signature of sublandlord)*

for the Sublandlord   ) The Sublandlord

)

_____) _____s

(signature of witness)   ) *(signature of subtenant)*

for the Subtenant   ) The Subtenant

FORM 909

10
ASSIGNMENTS

Form 1000. Assignment with warranties

Use this form for the general setup of a simple assignment *with* warranties.

An assignment is used for the transfer of the benefit of legal rights (e.g., the benefit of a contract). Note that the Assignor should also give the person owing the obligation involved in the legal right notice of the assignment in order to ensure the person directs the subsequent benefit of the legal right to the Assignee.

Remember there must be a right to make the assignment in order for the assignment to work. For example, in lease situations, the landlord often restricts the right to assign the lease without the landlord's consent.

Insert the description of subject matter of assignment in the first paragraph in the proper space.

Form 1001. Assignment without warranties

Use this form the general setup of a simple assignment *without* warranties.

Insert the description of subject matter of assignment in the first paragraph in the proper space.

Form 1002. Assignment of money due

Use this form to assign money due under a simple statement of account. Note provisions for optional acknowledgment of notice of the assignment by the person owing the money.

Form 1003. Assignment of real estate contract

Use this form to assign the purchaser's benefit of an agreement of purchase and sale of real property. Insert description of property in the first paragraph in the proper space.

Form 1004. Assignment of contract

Use this form, with proper legal advice, to assign the general benefit of a contract (e.g., a car lease).

Form 1005. Assignment of copyright

Use this form to assign the copyright in some original writing. Notice of the assignment is not necessary where the "author" of the writing is the Assignor.

Form 1006. Notice of assignment

Use this form to give notice of an assignment to the person under the legal obligation in connection with the assigned contract/debt.

Form 1007. Check endorsements

Use these examples to draft check endorsements which, in effect, assign the payment benefit of a check. Write what is indicated on the back of the check. Each signature is, of course, the signature of the person to whom the check is originally made out — the Payee. The person receiving the endorsed check can re-endorse it over to someone else.

Note that you cannot re-endorse a check that is payable only to a named person.

ASSIGNMENT WITH WARRANTIES

For value received, which is acknowledged, _____
(assignor name)

(the "Assignor") hereby assigns all interest owned in _____

_____
(subject of assignment)

to _____ (the "Assignee").
(assignee name)

The Assignor also warrants to the Assignee that the Assignor owns the subject matter of this assignment and has the right to make this assignment without the consent of any third party.

Given under seal on _____.
(date)

Signed, sealed, and   )
delivered in the presence   )
of:)
)
)
_____   )   _____s
(signature of witness)   )   (signature of assignor)
for the Assignor   )   The Assignor

FORM 1000

ASSIGNMENT WITHOUT WARRANTIES

For value received, which is acknowledged, _____
(assignor name)

_____ (the "Assignor")

hereby assigns all interest owned in _____
(subject of assignment)

to _____ (the "Assignee").
(assignee name)

The Assignor stipulates, however, that this assignment is made completely at the risk of the Assignee without any representations, warranties, or collateral assurances of any kind whatsoever with regard to the subject matter of this assignment, its ownership, or the right to make this assignment.

Given under seal on _____.
(date)

Signed, sealed, and	)	
delivered in the presence	)	
of:	)	
	)	
_____	)	_____s
(signature of witness)	)	*(signature of assignor)*
for the Assignor	)	The Assignor

FORM 1001

ASSIGNMENT OF MONEY DUE

For value received, which is acknowledged, _____ (the "Assignor")
                                              (assignor name)
hereby assigns all interest and benefit in the attached statement of account (the "Account")

_____

to _____ (the "Assignee").
                (assignee name)

The Assignor warrants to the Assignee that:

    a) the Account is due and owing in its full face amount;

    b) no payment has been made on the Account; and,

    c) there is no defence to or right of set-off or counterclaim against the Account.

Given under seal on _____
                            (date)

Signed, sealed, and   )
delivered in the presence   )
of:)
)
_____) _____s
(signature of witness)   ) *(signature of assignor)*
for the Assignor   ) The Assignor

The undersigned acknowledges notice of and consents to the above assignment.

Dated_____

Witnessed By:)
)
_____) _____s
(signature of witness)   ) *(signature of debtor)*

FORM 1002

ASSIGNMENT OF REAL ESTATE CONTRACT

For value received, which is acknowledged, _____ (the "Assignor")
(assignor name)

hereby assigns all interest and benefit in an agreement of purchase and sale of

_____ between

_____ (the "Vendor")
(vendor name)

and the Assignor, accepted by the Vendor on _____

(date)

to _____ (the "Assignee").
(assignee name)

The Assignor stipulates, however, that this assignment is made completely at the risk of the Assignee without any representations, warranties or collateral assurances of any kind whatsoever with regard to the subject matter of this assignment, its ownership, or the right to make this assignment.

Given under seal on _____.
(date)

Signed, sealed, and   )
delivered in the presence   )
of:)
)
_____   ) _____s
(signature of witness)   ) *(signature of assignor)*
for the Assignor   ) The Assignor

FORM 1003

140

ASSIGNMENT OF CONTRACT

For value received, which is acknowledged, _____
                                                                    (assignor name)

_____ (the "Assignor")

hereby assigns all interest and benefit in the attached contract to _____
                                                                                              (assignee name)

_____ (the "Assignee").

The Assignor stipulates, however, that this assignment is made completely at the risk of the Assignee without any representations, warranties, or collateral assurances of any kind whatsoever with regard to the subject matter of this assignment, its ownership, or the right to make this assignment.

Given under seal on _____.
                                    (date)

Signed, sealed, and   )
delivered in the presence   )
of:)
)
_____   )   _____s
(signature of witness)   )   *(signature of assignor)*
for the Assignor   )   The Assignor

FORM 1004

ASSIGNMENT OF COPYRIGHT

For value received, which is acknowledged, _____
(assignor name)

(the "Assignor") hereby assigns all copyright in _____
(name of work)

(the "Work") to _____ (the "Assignee").
(assignee name)

The Assignor warrants to the Assignee that:

    a) copyright exists in the Work;

    b) the Assignor owns all the copyright in the Work;

    c) the Assignor has the right to assign the copyright in the Work;

    d) there is no dispute or pending dispute over the existence or ownership of copyright in the Work;

    e) the Assignee can register and dispose of the copyright in the Work in the Assignee's own name.

Given under seal on_____.
                    (date)

Signed, sealed, and   )
delivered in the presence   )
of:)
)
_____) _____s
(signature of witness)   ) *(signature of assignor)*
for the Assignor   ) The Assignor

FORM 1005

142

NOTICE OF ASSIGNMENT

January 1, 199-

Any Company
12 Any Street
Anytown, Anystate
12345

Dear _____

Re Notice of Assignment

This is to notify you that I have legally assigned all interest and benefit in _____

_____
              (subject matter)

to _____
              (name)

of _____
              (address)

effective _____.
              (date)

Please direct yourself to the named assignee accordingly.

Very truly yours,

_____
(signature)

FORM 1006

143

CHECK ENDORSEMENTS

[TO PAY ANY HOLDER OF THE ENDORSED CHECK]

_____
(signature of payee)

[TO PAY A NAMED PERSON OR ACCORDING TO HIS/HER
SUBSEQUENT ENDORSEMENT]

Pay _____or Order. _____
          (name)   *(signature of payee)*

[TO PAY ONLY A NAMED PERSON (SAFEST ENDORSEMENT)]

Pay _____only. _____
          (name)   *(signature of payee)*

FORM 1007

144

11
CORPORATE

Form 1100. Notice of annual meeting of shareholders

The general by-laws of a corporation usually require proper notice to be given of a meeting of shareholders. Use this form to give formal notice of an annual meeting of shareholders.

Form 1101. Notice of special meeting of shareholders

Use this form to give formal notice of any shareholders' meeting other than the annual meeting. Attach a copy of the draft resolution as Schedule 1. This draft resolution should be self-explanatory of the nature of the special business to be transacted at the meeting.

Form 1102. Proxy form

Use this form to appoint a non-solicited proxy to attend and vote in your place at a shareholders' meeting.

Note that many jurisdictions have special rules governing solicited proxies.

Form 1103. Notice of meeting of directors

The general by-laws of a corporation usually require proper notice to be given of a meeting of directors. Use this form to give formal notice of a meeting of directors.

Form 1104. Minutes of shareholders' meeting

Minutes should be kept of every formal meeting of shareholders or directors of a corporation. Use this form as a sample for formal minutes of a meeting of shareholders to be inserted in the corporate minute book.

Form 1105. Minutes of directors' meeting

Use this form as a sample for formal minutes of a meeting of directors to be inserted in the corporate minute book. The dissenting votes, if any, should be recorded for each motion.

Form 1106 and Form 1107. Shareholders' and directors' resolutions

Many small corporations are so closely held (few shareholders and directors) that going through the motions of sending out formal notice of a meeting, holding a meeting, and keeping formal minutes of that meeting is somewhat artificial. Use Form 1106 to prepare written, unanimously signed shareholders' resolutions and Form 1107 to prepare directors' resolutions instead. Remember to store the written resolutions in the corporate minute book.

Form 1108 and Form 1109. Sole shareholder's and sole director's resolutions

Some corporations have only one shareholder or one director. This makes going through the motions of sending out formal notice of a meeting, holding a formal meeting, and keeping minutes of the meeting somewhat artificial. Use Form 1108 to prepare written sole shareholder's resolutions and Form 1109 to prepare sole director's resolutions instead. Remember to store the written resolutions in the corporate minute book.

Form 1110 and Form 1111. Waivers of notice

Sometimes meetings of shareholders or directors are held without formal notice but with everyone present who should be present. Use Form 1110 to formally record waiver of proper notice of a meeting of shareholders and Form 1111 to formally record waiver of proper notice of a meeting of directors.

Form 1112 and Form 1113. Resignations of officer and director

Use these forms to compose a formal letter of resignation by an officer (Form 1112) or director (Form 1113) of a corporation.

Form 1114. Audit legal information query

If your company's financial statements are audited, use this form to obtain your attorney's confirmation of no outstanding legal claims by or against the company.

Form 1115. By-law

By-laws are the internal rules governing the corporation. Use this form, with proper legal advice, to draft a corporate by-law or amending by-law. Note that the by-law is passed by the directors and confirmed by the shareholders.

Form 1116. Share subscription

Use this form to draft a formal subscription for issuance of shares of a corporation.

Form 1117. Acceptance of directorship

Directors are elected by shareholders but, occasionally, there is some doubt as to whether the person elected agreed to ac-cept the office. Use this form to document a person's acceptance of office.

Form 1118. Corporate organizing resolutions

Use this form, with proper legal advice, to draft the initial organizing resolutions of a corporation.

Form 1119. Annual directors' resolutions

Use this form, with proper legal advice, to draft annual directors' resolutions.

Form 1120. Other directors' resolutions

This form illustrates some typical written directors' resolutions.

Form 1121. Annual shareholders' resolutions

Use this form, with proper legal advice, to draft annual shareholders' resolutions.

Form 1122. Other shareholders' resolutions

This form illustrates some typical written shareholders' resolutions.

Form 1123. Certificate of true copy

Use this form where a certificate of some corporate action is required.

Form 1124. Assignment of share

Use this form to draft an assignment of a share.

NOTICE OF ANNUAL MEETING OF SHAREHOLDERS

_____
(corporate name)

Notice is hereby given that the Annual Meeting of shareholders of_____
(the "Corporation")

_____
will be held on_____at_____
(date)   (address)

_____
commencing at_____for the following purposes:
(time)

    a) to receive the financial statements of the Corporation for the fiscal year ended

    _____.
    (date)

    [OPTIONAL:] together with the reports of the auditors and directors on the statements,

    and to appoint auditors for the current fiscal year of the Corporation];

    b) to elect directors for the Corporation;

    c) to transact any other business that may properly come before the meeting and any adjournments.

Dated at _____on_____.
(place)   (date)

By Order of the Board of Directors

_____
(signature of secretary)

_____
(secretary name, typed)

Corporate Secretary

FORM 1100

NOTICE OF SPECIAL MEETING OF SHAREHOLDERS

_____
(corporate name)

Notice is hereby given that a Special Meeting of shareholders of_____

(the "Corporation")

_____

will be held on_____at_____

(date)   *(address)*

_____

commencing at_____for the following purposes:

(time)

    a) to consider passage of the resolution appended to this notice as Schedule 1;

    b) to transact any other business that may properly come before the meeting and any adjournments.

Dated at _____on_____.

(place)   *(date)*

By Order of the Board of Directors

_____

(signature of secretary)

_____

(secretary name, typed)

Corporate Secretary

FORM 1101

PROXY FORM

_____
(corporate name)

The undersigned shareholder of_____
(corporate name)

hereby appoints_____
(proxy name)

as the nominee of the undersigned to attend and act for the undersigned at the meeting of shareholders of the corporation to be held on _____
(date)

at _____
(address)

and at any adjournments of that meeting in the same manner and with the same power, including with respect to voting, as the undersigned if the undersigned were present in person.

Dated _____.
(date)

_____
(signature of witness)
Witness

_____
(signature of shareholder)

_____
(shareholder name, typed)

FORM 1102

NOTICE OF MEETING OF DIRECTORS

_____
(corporate name)

Notice is hereby given that a meeting of the Board of Directors of

_____
(corporate name)

will be held on_____at_____
(date)

_____
(address)

commencing at_____.
(time)

Dated at_____on_____.
(place)   (date)

By Order of the Board of Directors

_____
(signature of secretary)

_____
(secretary name, typed)

Corporate Secretary

FORM 1103

MINUTES OF SHAREHOLDERS' MEETING

_____
(corporate name)

A meeting of shareholders of _____
(corporate name)

was duly called and held on _____ at _____
(date)

_____
(address)

commencing at_____.
(time)

With the approval of the shareholders present, _____
(chair name)

acted as Chair of the meeting and _____
(secretary name)

recorded the minutes.

The Chair noted that the required quorum of shareholders was present to conduct business and that the meeting was properly constituted.

On motions duly made and seconded, it was voted that:

1. The minutes of the last meeting of shareholders be taken as read.

2. _(insert resolution per numbered paragraph)_

There being no further business to transact at this time, it was voted to adjourn the meeting.

Dated_____.
(date)

_____   _____
(signature of secretary)   (signature of chair)

_____   _____
(secretary name, typed)   (chair name, typed)
Secretary   Chair

FORM 1104

MINUTES OF DIRECTORS' MEETING

_____
(corporate name)

Minutes of a meeting of the Board of Directors of_____
(corporate name)

duly called and held on_____at _____
(date)

_____
(address)

commencing at_____ .
(time)

Present were:

With the approval of the directors present, _____
(chair name)

acted as Chair of the meeting and _____
(secretary name)

recorded the minutes.

On motions duly made and seconded, it was voted that:

1. The minutes of the last meeting of directors be taken as read.

2. *(insert resolution per numbered paragraph)*

Dissenting to the motion were

_____

_____

_____
(dissenting names)

There being no further business to transact at this time, it was voted to adjourn the meeting.

Dated _____ .
(date)

_____   _____
(signature of secretary)   *(signature of chair)*

_____   _____
(secretary name, typed)   *(chair name, typed)*

Secretary   Chair

FORM 1105

SHAREHOLDERS' RESOLUTIONS

The undersigned, being all the voting shareholders of

_____,
                              (corporate name)

hereby sign the following resolutions:

RESOLVED THAT

    1.   *(insert resolution per numbered paragraph)*

Dated _____.
            (date)

_____   _____
(signature of shareholder)   *(signature of shareholder)*

_____   _____
(shareholder name, typed)   *(shareholder name, typed)*

FORM 1106

The undersigned, being all the directors of

_____/

(corporate name)

hereby sign the following resolutions:

RESOLVED THAT

    1.   *(insert resolution per numbered paragraph)*

Dated _____.

           (date)

_____	_____
(signature of director)	*(signature of director)*
_____	_____
(director name, typed)	*(director name, typed)*

FORM 1107

SOLE SHAREHOLDER'S RESOLUTIONS

The undersigned sole shareholder of

_____,
(corporate name)

hereby signs the following resolutions:

RESOLVED THAT

    1.   *(insert resolution per numbered paragraph).*

Dated _____.
              (date)

_____
(signature of shareholder)

_____
(shareholder name, typed)

FORM 1108

The undersigned sole director of

_____
(corporate name)

hereby signs the following resolutions:

RESOLVED THAT

   1.   *(insert resolution per numbered paragraph)*

Dated _____.
            (date)

_____
(signature of director)

_____
(director name, typed)

FORM 1109

SHAREHOLDER'S WAIVER OF NOTICE

The undersigned shareholder in_____
(corporate name)

hereby waives proper notice of the meeting of shareholders held on_____
(date)

at_____,
(address)

commencing at_____.
(time)

Dated _____.
(date)

_____
(signature of shareholder)

_____
(shareholder name, typed)

FORM 1110

DIRECTOR'S WAIVER OF NOTICE

The undersigned director of _____
                                            (corporate name)

hereby waives proper notice of the meeting of directors held on _____
                                                                        (date)

at _____
                                (address)

commencing at_____.
                          (time)

Dated _____.
              (date)

_____
(signature of director)

_____
(director name, typed)

FORM 1111

158

RESIGNATION OF OFFICER

To: _____
    (corporate name)

Re Resignation of Office

I hereby resign as _____
                         (office)

of _____
    (corporate name)

effective immediately.

Dated _____.
         (date)

Very truly yours,

_____
(signature of resigning officer)

_____
(resigning officer name, typed)

FORM 1112

159

RESIGNATION OF DIRECTOR

To: _____
         (corporate name)

Re Resignation of Directorship

I hereby resign as a director of _____
                                      (corporate name)

effective immediately.

Dated _____.
              (date)

Very truly yours,

_____
(signature of director)

_____
(director name, typed)

FORM 1113

AUDIT LEGAL INFORMATION QUERY

January 1, 199-
Any Company Ltd.
12 Any Street
Anytown, Anystate
12345

Dear _____:

Re Audit Legal Information Query

Our auditors are presently engaged in the preparation of audited financial statements for our fiscal year ended_____.
(date)

We have determined that there were no legal claims or possible legal claims outstanding by or against the company as of_____.
(date)

Please confirm that your law firm acts for the company and that there are no such claims with respect to which your law firm's advice or representation has been sought.

If you are aware of any such claims, please state the names of the parties to and the amount involved in each such claim.

Please address your reply to this company "Privileged & Confidential" and send a signed copy of your letter directly to our auditors,

_____,
(name of auditors)

at _____.
(address)

Very truly yours,

_____
(signature)

copy to

_____

_____

(name of auditors)

FORM 1114

161

_____

(corporate name)

By-Law No._____

(number)

A by-law to _____.

Be it enacted as By-Law No._____

(number)

of _____,

(corporate name)

(the "Corporation") that:

The directors and officers of the Corporation are instructed and authorized to take such action and execute such instruments as are required or deemed advisable to implement this by-law.

Passed by the undersigned, being all the directors of _____

(corporate name)

on_____.

(date)

_____   _____

(signature of director)   (signature of director)

_____   _____

(director name, typed)   (director name, typed)

Confirmed by the undersigned, being all the shareholders of_____,

(corporate name)

on_____.

(date)

_____   _____

(signature of shareholder)   (signature of shareholder

_____   _____

(shareholder name, typed)   (shareholder name, typed)

FORM 1115

SHARE SUBSCRIPTION

The undersigned hereby subscribes for_____
(number and class of shares)

share(s) of the authorized share capital of _____
(corporate name)

and tenders the sum of $ _____ for issuance of the shares as fully paid up.

Dated _____.
(date)

_____
(signature of subscriber)

_____
(subscriber name, typed)

FORM 1116

ACCEPTANCE OF DIRECTORSHIP

The undersigned hereby accepts the office of director of _____
                                                                    (corporate name)
effective on election.

Dated _____.
                (date)

_____
(signature of director)

_____
(director name, typed)

FORM 1117

CORPORATE ORGANIZING RESOLUTIONS

DIRECTORS' RESOLUTIONS

The undersigned, being all the directors of_____,

(corporate name)

hereby sign the following organizing resolutions:

RESOLVED THAT

1. By-Law No. 1 is passed as the general by-law of the corporation to be placed before a meeting of shareholders of the corporation for confirmation.

2. The form(s) of share certificate(s) appended as Schedule A to these resolutions are adopted as the form(s) of share certificate(s) for the issued shares of the corporation.

3. The corporation issue the share(s) subscribed for in the signed share subscription(s) appended as Schedule B to these resolutions for the subscription price(s) set out.

4. The corporation have and the following person(s) are appointed to the following office(s):

   President : _____
   (president name)

   Vice-President :_____
   (vice-president name)

   Secretary :_____
   (secretary name)

   Treasurer :_____
   (treasurer name)

   Secretary-Treasurer :_____
   (secretary-treasurer name)

   Manager:_____.
   (manager name)

5. The corporate seal impressed in the margin of these resolutions is adopted as the corporate seal of the corporation.

6. _____is appointed the bank of the corporation in the completed form of banking resolution required by the bank and appended as Schedule C to these resolutions.

7. By-Law No. *(number)* is passed as the borrowing by-law of the corporation to be placed before a meeting of shareholders of the corporation for confirmation.

Dated _____

(date)

_____
(signature of director)

_____
(signature of director)

_____
(director name, typed)

_____
(director name, typed)

FORM 1118

SHAREHOLDERS' RESOLUTIONS

The undersigned, being all the shareholders of_____,
(corporate name)

hereby sign the following organizing resolutions:

RESOLVED THAT

1. These resolutions are in place of the first annual meeting of shareholders of the corporation.

_____   _____
    (names of directors)

2. are elected as all the directors of the corporation.

3. No auditor be appointed for the current fiscal year of the corporation.

[OR]

3. _____   _____
    (auditor names)

are appointed the auditors of the corporation for the current fiscal year.

4. By-Law No. 1 passed by the Board of Directors of the corporation is confirmed.

Dated _____.
    (date)

_____   _____
(signature of shareholder)   *(signature of shareholder)*

_____   _____
(shareholder name, typed)   *(shareholder name, typed)*

FORM 1118

ANNUAL DIRECTORS' RESOLUTIONS

The undersigned, being all the directors of_____,
                                                    (corporate name)

hereby sign the following resolutions:

RESOLVED THAT

1. The financial statements of the corporation for the fiscal year ended
    _____ prepared by_____,
            (date)   (accountants)

    chartered accountants, under their comments dated_____
                                                              (date)

    are approved which approval shall be evidenced by signature of the balance
    sheet.

[OR]

1. The financial statements of the corporation for the fiscal year ended
    _____prepared by _____
            (date)   (auditors)

    under their audit report dated_____ are approved, which
                                          (date)

    approval shall be evidenced by signature of the balance sheet.

2. The approved financial statements be placed before the annual meeting of
    shareholders of the corporation.

3. _____are appointed the accountants of the corporation
           (accountants)

    for the current fiscal year.

Dated _____.
              (date)

_____   _____
(signature of director)   (signature of director)

_____   _____
(director name, typed)   (director name, typed)

RESOLVED THAT

1. By-Law No. _____ is passed as a by-law of the corporation to be placed before a meeting of shareholders of the corporation for confirmation.

2. The application to amend the Articles of Incorporation [OR Letters Patent] of the corporation in the draft form appended as Schedule A to these resolutions is approved to be placed before a meeting of shareholders of the corporation for confirmation.

3. The corporation sell substantially all its assets to _____ in
   (name)

   accordance with the draft agreement of purchase and sale appended as Schedule A to these resolutions.

4. _____ is elected as Chair of the Board of
   (chair name)
   Directors.

5. A dividend of $_____ per share is declared on
   the issued_____ shares of the corporation held by the
   (class name)

   _____ shareholders of record as of this date.
   (class name)

6. The salary of the _____ of the corporation is fixed at
   (officer)

   $_____ per annum effective _____
   (date)

7. The corporation execute the _____ in the
   (contract/instrument)
   draft form appended as Schedule A to these resolutions.

8. The transfer of _____ from_____ to
   (number and class of shares)   (name)
   _____ is approved.
   (name)

9. The address of the head/registered office of the corporation is changed to

   _____.

   (address)

FORM 1120

ANNUAL SHAREHOLDERS' RESOLUTIONS

'The undersigned, being all the shareholders of _____ ,
                                                        (corporate name)

hereby sign the following annual resolutions:

RESOLVED THAT

1. These resolutions are in place of an annual meeting of shareholders of the corporation.

2. The financial statements of the corporation for the fiscal year ended _____, prepared by _____
    (date)   *(accountants)*

    Chartered Accountants, under their comments dated _____,
                                                              (date)

    are received.

                                    [OR]

2. The financial statements of the corporation for the fiscal year ended
    _____ prepared by _____,
    (date)   *(auditors)*

    under their audit report dated_____, are approved.
                                              (date)

3. _____and _____are continued as
      (director's name)   *(director's name)*

    directors of the corporation.

4. No auditor be appointed for the current fiscal year of the corporation.

                                    [OR]

4. _____ are appointed the auditors of
                      (auditors)

    the corporation for the current fiscal year.

5. The acts of the Board of Directors since the last annual meeting of shareholders are approved and ratified.

Dated_____.
              (date)

_____   _____
(signature of shareholder)   *(signature of shareholder)*

_____   _____
(shareholder name, typed)   *(shareholder name, typed)*

                                                            FORM 1121

RESOLVED THAT

1. _____ is elected as a director of the corporation.

     (director name)

2. By-Law No. _____ passed by the Board of Directors of the corporation is confirmed.

3. The application to amend the Articles of Incorporation [OR Letters Patent] of the corporation in the draft form appended as Schedule A to these resolutions is approved.

4. The proposed sale by the corporation of substantially all its assets to_____
   _____ in accordance with the draft agreement of

     (purchaser name)

   purchase and sale appended as Schedule A to these resolutions is approved.

5. _____ is removed as a director of the corporation.

     (director name)

FORM 1122

CERTIFICATE OF TRUE COPY

_____
(corporate name)

CERTIFICATE

The undersigned Secretary of _____
(corporate name)

hereby certifies that Schedule A appended to this certificate is a true copy of a _____
_____
(describe instrument)

passed by the shareholders [OR directors] of the corporation on _____.
(date)

Certified by me under the corporate seal of the corporation on _____.
(date)

_____c/s
(signature of secretary)

_____
(secretary name, typed),
Secretary

FORM 1123

ASSIGNMENT OF SHARE

For value received, which is acknowledged, _____
                                                (assignor name)

(the "Assignor") hereby assigns all interest and benefit to _____
                                                              (assignee name)

(the "Assignee") in the_____shares of _____
                          (class)   *(corporate name)*

evidenced by Share Certificate No(s)_____
                                            (numbers)

(the "Shares").

The Assignor warrants the Assignee that the Shares are fully paid up and that the Assignor owns the Shares free and clear of all encumbrances.

Given under seal on _____
                              (date)

Signed, sealed and   )
delivered in the presence   )
of:-   )
)
_____   )   _____s
(signature of witness)   )   *(signature of assignor)*
for the Assignor   )   The Assignor

FORM 1124

12
ESTATE PLANNING

Form 1200. Simple will leaving estate to spouse or children

Use this form, with proper legal advice and supervision of execution of the will, to prepare a simple will leaving everything to your spouse, but if he or she predeceases you, leaving everything to your children.

The person making the will is a "testator" if male and a "testatrix" if female. The person administering the estate is an "executor" if male and an "executrix" if female. Choose the appropriate gender form when making out the will.

Generally, a will has to be signed in front of two witnesses who attest the execution with their own signatures in front of the person making the will. Note that a witness cannot be a beneficiary under the will.

Residents of Washington and Oregon will find more information on wills and estate planning in *Wills for Washington* and *Wills and Estate Planning Handbook for Oregon,* also published by Self-Counsel Press.

Form 1201. Simple general will

Use this form, with proper legal advice and supervision of execution of the will, to prepare a simple general will. In section 3(b) and 3(c), list the seperate items or amounts you wish to leave to specific beneficiaries. Identify each item clearly.

Remember to always include a "residuary" beneficiary clause. Think of it as a catchall to cover anything you have not specifically named in the will. Otherwise, you may trigger a "partial intestacy" on any property you own that is not specifi-

cally dealt with. If you name a group of people as residuary beneficiaries, make sure you describe the group clearly. For example, "my children" is a clear description, but "my family" or "my relatives" is not.

Form 1202. Amendment to will (codicil)

Use this form, with proper legal advice and supervision of execution of the codicil, to make simple changes to your will. Keep the codicil simple; if the amendment is not simple, consider rewriting the will instead.

Form 1203. Estate information sheet

It is often difficult for an executor or executrix to administer an unfamiliar estate. Use this form to leave your executor or executrix information about your funeral wishes and the location of estate assets. Keep the completed form with your private papers.

Note that this form does not in any way take the place of a proper, legally executed will or codicil to a will.

Form 1204. Power of attorney with limitations

A power of attorney gives someone else authority to act and sign instruments in your name and on your behalf. It is a dangerous delegation of authority and should not be given lightly. Use this form, with proper legal advice, to give someone your power of attorney with limitations.

Form 1205. Power of attorney for real estate transactions

Use this form, with proper legal advice, to give someone your power of attorney for real estate paper signing. Under conditions and restrictions, choose and fill in either "purchase" or "sale" of the property.

Form 1206. Revocation of power of attorney

Use this form to revoke a power of attorney. Note that giving someone proof of power of attorney clothes him or her with apparent authority and that, in order to be effective, any revocation of that power must be communicated to anyone dealing with the attorney as an attorney and before he or she enters into anything binding with your attorney. Just signing this form or delivering it after the fact won't do it.

SIMPLE WILL LEAVING ESTATE TO SPOUSE OR CHILDREN

This is the last will of _____
(testator/testatrix name)

of the_____of_____
(municipality, city)   (place name)

in the State of _____.
(state)

1. I revoke all wills and testamentary dispositions previously made by me.

[HUSBAND LEAVING TO WIFE]

2. I give all my property to my spouse, _____,
(spouse name)

and appoint her my sole Executrix but, if she is unable or unwilling to act or to continue to act as my Executrix for any reason, then I appoint_____
_____,my sole Executor/Executrix instead
(alternate executor/executrix name)

and, if my spouse predeceases me or, surviving me, dies within thirty days of the date of my death, give all my property to be divided among my children alive at the date of the death of the survivor of my spouse and me in equal shares per capita.

[WIFE LEAVING TO HUSBAND]

2. I give all my property to my spouse,_____ ,
(spouse name)

and appoint him my sole Executor but, if he is unable or unwilling to act or to continue to act as my Executor for any reason, then I appoint_____
_____ ,my sole Executor/Executrix
(alternate executor/executrix name)

instead and, if my spouse predeceases me or, surviving me, dies within thirty days of the date of my death, give all my property to be divided among my children alive at the date of the death of the survivor of my spouse and me in equal shares per capita.

3. If any person becomes entitled to a share or interest in my estate before reaching the age of majority, my Executor/Executrix shall hold the share or interest and keep it invested until that person reaches the age of majority. Any income derived from the share or interest shall be added to it. However, my Executor/Executrix may apply so much of the capital and income for the benefit of the person while under the age of majority as my Executor/Executrix considers necessary or advisable in my Executor's/Executrix's absolute discretion. In this regard, my Executor/Executrix may make payments for the benefit of the person under the age of majority to any parent or guardian of the property of the person or anyone else standing in loco parentis to the person and the receipt of any such payee is a sufficient discharge to my Executor/Executrix for any such payment.

FORM 1200

4. Any reference to a beneficiary in this will or any codicil solely in terms of a relationship determined by blood or marriage does not include anyone born outside marriage or tracing their relationship through a person born outside marriage. However, anyone who is legally adopted before my death shall be deemed to have been born inside marriage to the adopting parents or parent and anyone born outside marriage whose natural parents marry before my death shall be deemed to have been born inside marriage to those parents.

5. In addition to any other powers conferred by this will and any codicil or by law, the person administering my estate or trusts may in his or her absolute discretion:

   a) realize any part of my estate not consisting of money at any time or times and in any manner and upon any terms, whether for cash or credit or part cash and part credit or postpone its realization for any length of time or retain it in the form in which it is at my death;

   b) make and change investments for my estate without being limited to investments authorized by law for trustees;

   c) exercise any rights, powers, and privileges and take or join in any action in connection with any investment in a corporation held from time to time in my estate that I could if I were alive and the sole owner of such investment;

   d) make any division of my estate or set aside or pay any share or interest in it, either wholly or in part, in the assets held from time to time in my estate; provided that the person shall fix the value of my estate or any part of it for the purpose of making any such division, setting aside, or payment; any value fixed by the person administering my estate or trusts pursuant to this power is in the absolute discretion of such person and final and binding on all persons concerned; notwithstanding any such division, setting aside, or payment, the person administering my estate or trusts is entitled to be compensated on the same basis as if the assets were sold and the proceeds dealt with in accordance with this will and any codicil;

   e) lease any real or leasehold property forming part of my estate from month to month, year to year, or for any term of months or years and subject to any covenants and conditions, accept surrenders of leases of the property, expend money on repairs and improvements to the property, generally manage the property, give any option with a view to sale of the property, and renew or pay off any mortgages on the property;

   f) borrow money on behalf of my estate upon any terms and conditions and mortgage, pledge, or otherwise charge any of the assets of my estate for any term for the repayment of the money borrowed;

FORM 1200

176

g) carry on any business which I may own or in which I may be interested at the time of my death, either alone or in partnership with one or more other persons, for any length of time.

In witness to which will, I have signed my name to it below on_____ .
(date)

Signed by the Testator/Testatrix in our   )

presence and by us in _____)
(his, her)

presence and in the presence   )

of each other:-   )

)

)   _____

)   *(testator/testatrix signature)*

Witness 1:_____   )
(signature)

_____   )

(printed name)   )

Address:_____   )

_____   )

Occupation:_____   )

)

Witness 2:_____   )
(signature)

_____   )

(printed name)   )

Address:_____   )

_____   )

Occupation:_____   )

FORM 1200

177

SIMPLE GENERAL WILL

This is the last will of _____
                                  (testator/testatrix name)

of the_____of_____
         (municipality, city)   *(place name)*

in the State of _____.
                              (state)

1. I revoke all wills and testamentary dispositions previously made by me.

2. I appoint_____
                    (first choice executor/executrix name)

    my sole_____but, if_____ is unable or
              (executor, executrix)   *(he, she)*

    unwilling to act or to continue to act for any reason, then I appoint

    _____
              (second choice executor/executrix name)

    my sole_____ instead.
              (executor, executrix)

3. I give all my property to my _____
                                          (executor, executrix)

    to deal with as follows:

    a) to pay my debts, funeral and testamentary expenses;

    b) to give the following items or property to the following
        persons:

        i)   my_____
                     (describe item/property)

              to _____
                     (recipient name);

FORM 1201

[ETC.]

c)   to pay the following amounts to the following persons:

i) $_____
(amount)

to_____
(recipient name);

[ETC.]

[INDIVIDUALLY NAMED RESIDUARY BENEFICIARIES]

d)   to give the residue of my estate to_____
(first choice residuary beneficiary name)

but, if_____predeceases me, to give it to_____
(he, she)

_____
(alternate residuary beneficiary name)

instead;

[GROUP DESCRIBED RESIDUARY BENEFICIARIES]

d)   to give the residue of my estate divided equally between those of_____

_____
(group description)

alive at the date of my death.

3.   If any person becomes entitled to a share or interest in my estate before reaching the age of majority, my Executor/Executrix shall hold the share or interest and keep it invested until that person reaches the age of majority. Any income derived from the share or interest shall be added to it. However, my Executor/Executrix may apply so much of the capital and income for the benefit of the person while under the age of majority as my Executor/Executrix considers necessary or advisable in my Executor's/Executrix's absolute discretion. In this regard, my Executor/Executrix may make payments for the benefit of the person under the age of majority to any parent or guardian of the property of the person or anyone else standing in loco parentis to the person and the receipt of any such payee is a sufficient discharge to my Executor/Executrix for any such payment.

4.   Any reference to a beneficiary in this will or any codicil solely in terms of a relationship determined by blood or marriage does not include anyone born outside marriage or tracing their relationship through a person born outside marriage. However, anyone who is legally adopted before my death shall be deemed to have been born inside marriage to the adopting parents or parent and anyone born outside marriage whose natural parents marry before my death shall be deemed to have been born inside marriage to those parents.

FORM 1201

5. In addition to any other powers conferred by this will and any codicil or by law, the person administering my estate or trusts may in his or her absolute discretion:

a) realize any part of my estate not consisting of money at any time or times and in any manner and upon any terms, whether for cash or credit or part cash and part credit or postpone its realization for any length of time or retain it in the form in which it is at my death;

b) make and change investments for my estate without being limited to investments authorized by law for trustees;

c) exercise any rights, powers, and privileges and take or join in any action in connection with any investment in a corporation held from time to time in my estate that I could if I were alive and the sole owner of such investment;

d) make any division of my estate or set aside or pay any share or interest in it, either wholly or in part, in the assets held from time to time in my estate; provided that the person shall fix the value of my estate or any part of it for the purpose of making any such division, setting aside, or payment; any value fixed by the person administering my estate or trusts pursuant to this power is in the absolute discretion of such person and final and binding on all persons concerned; notwithstanding any such division, setting aside, or payment, the person administering my estate or trusts is entitled to be compensated on the same basis as if the assets were sold and the proceeds dealt with in accordance with this will and any codicil;

e) lease any real or leasehold property forming part of my estate from month to month, year to year or for any term of months or years and subject to any covenants and conditions, accept surrenders of leases of the property, expend money on repairs and improvements to the property, generally manage the property, give any option with a view to sale of the property, and renew or pay off any mortgages on the property;

f) borrow money on behalf of my estate upon any terms and conditions and mortgage, pledge, or otherwise charge any of the assets of my estate for any term for the repayment of the money borrowed;

FORM 1201

180

g) carry on any business which I may own or in which I may be interested at the time of my death, either alone or in partnership with one or more other persons, for any length of time.

In witness to which will, I have signed my name to it below on_____
                                                                                                  (date)

Signed by the _____)
                        (testator, testatrix)   )
in our   )
presence and by us in _____)
                                    (his, her)   )
presence and in the presence   )
of each other:-   )
)   _____
)   *(testator/testatrix name)*

Witness 1:_____   )
                    (signature)   )
)
_____   )
                    (printed name)   )
Address:_____   )
_____   )
Occupation:_____   )
)
Witness 2:_____   )
                    (signature)   )
)
_____   )
                    (printed name)   )
Address:_____   )
_____   )
Occupation:_____   )

FORM 1201

181

CODICIL

This is the _____ codicil to the will dated _____
                  (first, second, third)   *(date)*

of_____of the_____
        (testator/testatrix name)   *(municipality, city)*

of_____ in the State of_____.
        (place name)   *(state)*

1. I revoke clause _____ of my will and substitute the following for it:
                            [INSERT NEW CLAUSE]

2. In all other respects I confirm my will.

In witness to which codicil, I have signed my name to it below on_____.
                                                                            (date)

Signed by the_____)
                    (testator, testatrix)   )
in our presence and by us in_____)
                                  (his, her)   )
presence and in the presence   )
of each other:-   )
)   _____
)   *(testator/testatrix signature)*
Witness 1:_____   )
                    (signature)   )
)

_____   )
            (printed name)   )
Address:_____   )
_____   )
Occupation:_____   )
)
Witness 2:_____   )
                    (signature)   )
)

_____   )
            (printed name)   )
Address:_____   )
_____   )
Occupation:_____   )

FORM 1202

ESTATE INFORMATION SHEET

NOTHING ON THIS FORM IS TO BE CONSIDERED A WILL OR A CODICIL TO A WILL OR AS AMENDING A PREVIOUSLY MADE WILL OR CODICIL TO A WILL

For Administering the Estate of: _____

Funeral Preference: _____

_____

_____

Other Non-Binding Estate Administration Wishes: _____

_____

_____

_____

_____

_____

Location of Bank Accounts/Safety Deposit Boxes: _____

_____

_____

_____

Location of Real Property Holdings: _____

_____

_____

_____

Location of Other Valuable Property/Papers: _____

_____

_____

_____

Other Helpful Estate Administration Information: _____

_____

_____

_____

_____

FORM 1203

_____

This power of attorney is given by_____of_____

(name of donor of power)

_____.

(address)

I hereby appoint_____of _____

(name of attorney)   _(address)_

to be my attorney and to do in my name and on my behalf anything that I can lawfully do by an attorney subject to the following conditions and restrictions:

[INSERT CONDITIONS AND RESTRICTIONS].

If permitted under the laws of this and any other applicable jurisdiction, I stipulate that this power of attorney remains in force during any subsequent legal incapacity of mine.

Given under seal on_____.

(date)

Signed, Sealed and   )

Delivered in the Presence   )

of:-   )

)

_____) _____s

(signature of witness))   )   _(signature of donor of power)_

) _____

FORM 1204

POWER OF ATTORNEY FOR REAL ESTATE TRANSACTIONS

This power of attorney is given by_____of_____
(name of donor of power)

_____.
(address)

I hereby appoint_____of _____
(name of attorney)   *(address)*

to be my attorney and to do in my name and on my behalf anything that I can lawfully do by an attorney subject to the following conditions and restrictions:

Limited to executing and swearing all instruments required in connection with my

_____of _____.
(purchase, sale)   *(property address)*

If permitted under the laws of this and any other applicable jurisdiction, I stipulate that this power of attorney remains in force during any subsequent legal incapacity of mine.

Given under seal on_____
(date)

Signed, Sealed and   )
Delivered in the Presence   )
of:-   )
)
)
_____   )   _____ s
(signature of witness)   )   *(signature of donor of power)*
)
)   _____
)   *(name of donor of power, typed)*

FORM 1205

REVOCATION OF POWER OF ATTORNEY

To Whom It May Concern

I hereby revoke the power of attorney given by me to _____

(name of attorney)

of _____

(address)

on_____effective immediately.

(date)

Dated: _____.

(date)

Witnessed By:)

)

_____   )

(signature of witness)   )   _____

)   *(signature of donor of power)*

)   _____

)   *(name of donor of power, typed)*

FORM 1206

13
REAL ESTATE

Form 1300. Contract clauses

Many real estate deals proceed on the basis of a preprinted standard offer/contract, often drawn up with the real estate agent, to which additional clauses may be added. This contract is the most important document in a real esate transaction as it defines everyone's rights. It should be taken to an attorney before signing.

Use the examples in this form, with proper legal advice, to draft additional clauses to be added to the preprinted standard offer/contract.

Form 1301. Interim occupancy agreement

Sometimes a real estate deal closing has to be extended but the purchaser nonetheless wants to take interim possession of the property on the date originally scheduled for closing. Use this form, with proper legal advice, to set up an interim possession arrangement.

Form 1302. Waiver of conditions

Many agreements of puchase and sale of real estate are conditional on something which may be difficult to pin down. Use this form to pin down the fulfillment of a condition by getting it waived.

a) PURCHASER FINANCING CONDITIONS

This agreement is conditional in favour of the purchaser on the purchaser arranging adequate financing to complete the purchase on acceptable terms to the purchaser.

This agreement is conditional on the purchaser notifying the vendor in writing within _____days of the date of this agreement that the purchaser has arranged adequate financing to complete the purchase on acceptable terms to the purchaser; failing such notice, this agreement is automatically void and the vendor shall immediately return any deposit paid by the purchaser without interest or deduction.

b) PURCHASER INSPECTION CONDITION

This agreement is conditional on the purchaser notifying the vendor in writing within _____days of the date of this agreement that the purchaser has obtained an inspection report satisfactory to the purchaser from a person chosen by the purchaser as to the condition of the building(s) on the subject property; failing such notice, this agreement is automatically void and the vendor shall immediately return any deposit paid by the purchaser without interest or deduction.

c) PURCHASER HOME SALE CONDITION

This agreement is conditional on the purchaser notifying the vendor in writing within _____days of the date of this agreement that the purchaser has entered into a binding agreement for the sale of the purchaser's property at_____; failing such notice, this agreement is automatically void and the vendor shall immediately return any deposit paid by the purchaser without interest or deduction. While the agreement is subject to this condition, the vendor may continue to advertise the subject property for sale and may require the purchaser by notice in writing to deliver a written waiver of this condition to the vendor within two days of the date of receipt of the notice; failing such delivery, this agreement is automatically void and the vendor shall immediately return any deposit paid by the purchaser without interest or deduction.

d) UNSPECIFIED PURCHASER CONDITION

This agreement is conditional on the purchaser notifying the vendor in writing within _____days of the date of this agreement that_____

_____

_____

(describe condition to be fulfilled)

failing such notice, this agreement is automatically void and the vendor shall immediately return any deposit paid by the purchaser without interest or deduction.

FORM 1300

INTERIM OCCUPANCY AGREEMENT

This interim occupancy agreement is made under seal between:

(1) _____ (the "Purchaser")
(name)

and

(2) _____ (the "Vendor").
(name)

Whereas the parties have executed the agreement of purchase and sale of certain property (the "Property") of which a copy is appended as Schedule A;

And whereas the parties wish to extend the closing date in Schedule A (the "Original Closing Date") but the Vendor is prepared to allow the Purchaser interim occupancy of the Property until closing;

It is agreed as follows:

1.   The closing date in Schedule A is extended to _____

(date)

(the "Extended Closing Date").

2.   The Purchaser shall pay _____ dollars ($_____) "Interim Payment") to the Vendor's lawyer in trust for the purposes set out in this agreement.

3.   The Vendor grants the Purchaser a purely contractual licence to occupy the Property on the terms set out in this agreement until twelve o'clock midnight on the Extended Closing Date. The Purchaser acknowledges that this grant of licence gives the Purchaser no leasehold or tenancy interest in the Property and accepts that the Purchaser occupies and brings personal property onto the Property entirely at the Purchaser's own risk.

4.   Notwithstanding the Extended Closing Date, the balance of the purchase price payable on closing for the Property provided for in Schedule A shall be adjusted as of the Original Closing Date. However, in addition to the purchase price, the Purchaser shall pay the Vendor on closing an amount equal to the interest accruing between the Original Closing Date and the Extended Closing Date on the Vendor's mortgage of the Property.

5.   If the agreement in Schedule A, as amended by this agreement, is not completed on the Extended Closing Date, the Purchaser:

a) covenants to quit and give the Purchaser immediate vacant possession of the Property in the same condition as on the Original Closing Date, reasonable wear and tear excepted;

b) covenants to pay the reasonable costs, if necessary, of restoring the Property to the same condition as on the Original Closing Date, reasonable wear and tear excepted;

FORM 1301

c) covenants not to invoke the protection of any landlord and tenant legislation against the Vendor seeking repossession of the Property;

d) guarantees that no third party occupying the Property with the Purchaser's consent will invoke the protection of any landlord and tenant legislation against the Vendor seeking repossession of the Property; and,

e) covenants to reimburse the Vendor for all costs, including but not limited to legal fees, reasonably incurred by the Vendor in recovering possession of the Property.

6. In any event, the Purchaser shall pay all water, electrical, and gas charges, as applicable, incurred in connection with the Purchaser's occupation of the Property.

7. If the agreement in Schedule A, as amended by this agreement, is not completed on the Extended Closing Date for any valid legal reason, the Vendor shall refund the Interim Payment without interest less, as applicable, the reasonable costs of restoring the Property to the same condition as on the Original Closing Date, reasonable wear and tear excepted, all water, electrical, and gas charges incurred in connection with the Purchaser's occupation of the Property and all costs, including but not limited to legal fees, reasonably incurred in recovering possession of the Property.

8. If the agreement in Schedule A, as amended by this agreement, is not completed by the Purchaser on the Extended Closing Date other than for a valid legal reason, the Vendor may take the Interim Payment as an occupancy charge for the Purchaser's occupation of the Property under this agreement without affecting the Purchaser's liability to complete the purchase of the Property or the Purchaser's other payment obligations under this agreement.

9. If any provision or part of any provision in this agreement is void or unenforceable for any reason, it shall be severed without affecting the validity of the balance of this agreement.

10. Time is of the essence of this agreement.

Executed in duplicate under seal on_____.

(date)

Signed, Sealed and	)	
Delivered in the Presence	)	
of:-	)	
_____	)	_____s
(signature of witness)	)	(signature of purchaser)
for the Purchaser	)	_____
	)	(purchaser name, typed)
_____	)	_____s
(signature of witness)	)	(signature of vendor)
for the Vendor)	)	_____
	)	(vendor name, typed)

FORM 1301

192

WAIVER OF CONDITIONS

PROPERTY: _____
(address)

VENDOR: _____
(name)

PURCHASER: _____
(name)

AGREEMENT: _____
(date)

The undersigned hereby waive(s) all conditions in the above agreement of purchase and sale.

Dated: _____.
(date)

Witnessed By:)
)
_____) _____
(signature of witness)) (signature)

FORM 1302

14
MISCELLANEOUS

Form 1400. Unilateral release of liability

Use this form to draft a unilateral (from one side) release of liability in connection with the final settlement of a potential claim against the other side.

Insert description of potential liability situation at end of first paragraph.

Form 1401. Mutual release of liability

Use this form to draft a mutual (by both sides) release of liabilities in connection with final settlement of mutual potential claims.

Insert description of potential mutual liability situation at end of first paragraph.

Form 1402. Trade secret non-disclosure agreement

Use this form, with proper legal advice, to exact a non-disclosure of trade secrets covenant from an associated independent business.

Form 1403. Declaration of trust

Occasionally, someone might want to hold property in other than his or her own name. The person in whose name the property is held usually holds it in secret trust but this can create problems of proof (e.g., where a secret trustee dies apparently owning the property) if there is nothing in writing. Use this form, with proper legal advice on the implications and effectiveness of using the device, to document a secret trust.

UNILATERAL RELEASE OF LIABILITY

In consideration of the payment of _____ dollars ($ _____),

receipt of which is acknowledged, _____ (the "Claimant")
  (claimant name)

hereby finally and irrevocably releases _____ (the "Payer")
  (payer name)

from all liability to the Claimant, and settles all actions or causes of action against the Payer, for damages, loss or injury sustained by the Claimant, however arising, present and future, known and unknown at this time, relating to:

If the Claimant has instituted any legal proceedings against the Payer settled by this release, the Claimant covenants to have them dismissed at the Claimant's cost with express prejudice to bringing further proceedings against the Payer arising out of the same matter.

The Claimant also covenants not to make any claim or institute any proceedings against any person who might claim over against or claim contribution or indemnity from the Payer in connection with any matter for which this release is given.

The Claimant also acknowledges that the Payer does not admit liability to the Claimant in connection with any matter for which this release is given.

Given under seal on _____.
  (date)

Signed, sealed, and   )
delivered in the presence   )
of:)
)
_____   ) _____ s
(signature of witness)   ) *(signature of claimant)*
for the Claimant   )

FORM 1400

195

MUTUAL RELEASE OF LIABILITY

The undersigned hereby finally and irrevocably mutually release each other from all liability to each other and settle all actions and causes of action against each other for damages, loss, or injury sustained by either of them, however arising, present and future, known and unknown at this time, relating to:

If either party has instituted any legal proceedings against the other settled by this release, that party covenants to have them dismissed at that party's cost with express prejudice to bringing further proceedings against the other arising out of the same matter.

It is agreed that neither party to this mutual release will make any claim or take any proceedings against any person who might claim over against or claim contribution or indemnity from the other party in connection with any matter for which this mutual release is given.

It is understood and agreed that nothing in this mutual release is to be construed as an admission of liability in connection with any matter for which this mutual release is given.

Executed in duplicate under seal on_____.
　　　　　　　　　　　　　　　　　　　　(date)

Signed, sealed, and　　　　　　　　　　)
delivered in the presence　　　　　　　)
of:　　　　　　　　　　　　　　　　　)
　　　　　　　　　　　　　　　　　　)
_____　)　_____s
(signature of witness)　　　　　　　)　*(signature of party one)*
　　　　　　　　　　　　　　　　　　)
_____　)　_____s
(signature of witness)　　　　　　　)　*(signature of party two)*

FORM 1401

196

TRADE SECRET NON-DISCLOSURE AGREEMENT

Whereas _____ (the "Confider")
          (confider name)

is prepared to disclose certain trade secrets relating to_____

_____ (the "trade secrets")
          (insert details)

to _____ (the "Confidant")
          (confidant name)

for mutual business purposes;

The Confidant hereby covenants:

    a) to protect the confidentiality of the trade secrets and not to disclose them to any third party;

    b) to exploit the trade secrets only for the Confider's and the Confidant's mutual business purposes and not to exploit them for the Confidant's sole business purposes.

The Confidant accepts that, if any part of these covenants is void or unenforceable for any reason, it shall be severed without affecting the validity of the balance of the covenants.

Given under seal on _____.
          (date)

Signed, sealed, and   )

delivered in the presence   )

of:)

)

_____   )   _____s

(signature of witness)   )   *(signature of confidant)*

for the Confidant

FORM 1402

DECLARATION OF TRUST

This declaration of trust is made by (1) _____ (the "Trustee")
                                         (trustee name)

in favor of (2) _____ (the "Beneficiary").
                           (beneficiary name)

The Trustee solemnly declares that he holds _____

_____ (the "Property")
                                   (list details)

in trust solely for the benefit of the Beneficiary.

The Trustee further promises the Beneficiary:

a) not to deal with the Property in any way, except to transfer it to the Beneficiary, without the instructions and consent of the Beneficiary; and,

b) to account to the Beneficiary for any money received by the Trustee, other than from Beneficiary, in connection with holding the Property.

Given under seal on _____.
                         (date)

Signed, sealed, and   )
delivered in the presence   )
of:)

_____   )   _____s
(signature of witness)   )   *(signature of trustee)*

FORM 1403

198